MAKING TUTUS

Amanda Hall

MAKING TUTUS

THE CROWOOD PRESS

Contents

Introduction

The purpose of this book

This book aims to guide people through the process of constructing a tutu. It came about after teaching tutu-making not only to college students and to parents whose children needed tutus to perform in their dance school productions or in competition, but also to people who sought out private tuition and travelled from all over the world to learn the skill. It became apparent that there was little if any literature on the subject of tutu-making, and this book aims to fill that gap.

Although I work as a costumier for professional companies, I am conscious that this book is likely to be used by students and those making costumes for dance schools or for their own use. The first few chapters illustrate the processes I use to make a tutu and bodice to a standard needed for professional performances. The book assumes you will be making a whole costume, but to make just a tutu plate or a bodice, turn to the relevant section and start there.

Although I have yet to meet someone I couldn't teach to make a tutu, as a project they are not easy. You will need basic hand and machine sewing skills, tenacity and time. One of the most noticeable differences between a professional and an amateur is speed, but this will improve with practice. If you follow the instructions closely, there is no reason you should not be able to produce a good result.

I trained as a costume-maker and costumes are quite different from fashion. They need to be robust enough to undergo the rigours of performance and they may need altering as a dancer grows or someone else needs to wear them. If costume-making is new to you, there may be some things that surprise you as you follow the instructions.

What is a tutu?

A tutu is the general term for the traditional costume usually worn by female ballet dancers. There are many different styles of tutu plate (the 'skirt' section) that have emerged over the years as a result of evolving fashions and advances in fabric technology.

The type of complete ballet costume we are concerned with in this book is made of three separate elements: the tutu plate, the bodice and the decorative sections. These three parts are generally made separately before being assembled into one complete costume.

The tutu plate

The tutu plate itself also consists of three elements:

- a basque, which is made of drill and extends below a waistband which sits on the natural waist. It acts as a carrier for the knicker. It is this area below the waist where the dancer will be supported if they are partnered, and it needs to fit closely. A basque should be 7.5cm deep for the average dancer; if making for a child, the basque should be shallower at around 5cm.
- the knicker, made of cotton bobbinet onto which the nets are stitched.

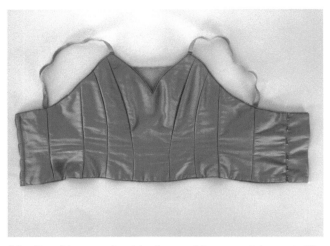

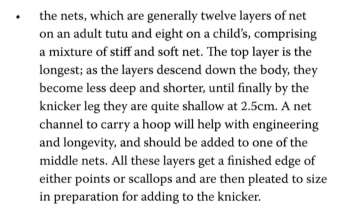

A tutu plate viewed from the underside.

A bodice, this example with a low neckline containing an infill.

- the nets, which are generally twelve layers of net on an adult tutu and eight on a child's, comprising a mixture of stiff and soft net. The top layer is the longest; as the layers descend down the body, they become less deep and shorter, until finally by the knicker leg they are quite shallow at 2.5cm. A net channel to carry a hoop will help with engineering and longevity, and should be added to one of the middle nets. All these layers get a finished edge of either points or scallops and are then pleated to size in preparation for adding to the knicker.

Once this tutu plate is assembled, the layers can be strung with thread to create different shapes:

A plate tutu – also known as a classical, pancake, dinner plate, platter or Russian tutu. These sit quite flat and create the iconic shape people generally bring to mind when they think of a tutu.

A drop tutu – also known as a bell or umbrella tutu, is a softer tutu and hangs in a domed shape.

There is a different type of ballet skirt which sometimes gets confused with a tutu. A romantic or Giselle ballet skirt is a long net skirt that was popularised in the early nineteenth century. They generally consist of around five or six layers of soft tulle and are stitched onto a long basque. They differ from a tutu as they don't have an integral knicker but are worn with separate frilled pants.

The bodice

The bodice is the upper part of the costume that finishes below the waist on the high hip line, or can end at the waist. It is devised in such a way as to allow the dancer as much movement as possible while still holding enough shape to echo the heavily boned and structured bodices of earlier fashions.

The decoration

Decorations tend to be constructed separately to the tutu and bodice sections and are stitched onto their own net bases, which are then applied to the costume before the sections are connected. These decorative elements help to bring the costume together as they often flow from the bodice onto the plate.

A brief history of the tutu

The tutu is a garment that developed in response to the emergence and increasing popularity of ballet, the classical form of dance which originated in the royal courts during the Italian Renaissance. The art form spread to France with Catherine de Medici and reached its peak at the time of Louis XIV during the seventeenth century. Ballet spread to Russia where it thrived in the nineteenth century and today many countries around the world have national ballet companies.

There were initially no special costumes; embellished traditional court dress was worn until the beginning of the eighteenth century when the skirt hem was raised slightly to display the feet. Towards the end of that century, the image of the female dancer we know today began to emerge as a romantic, feminine ideal.

The design of the tutu has been credited to artist Eugène Lami and Swedish-born dancer Marie Taglioni who first wore it at the premiere of *La Sylphide* at Paris Opéra Ballet in 1832. Her muslin bell-shaped ballet skirt was shortened to a level which fell halfway between the knee and the ankle, and not only helped portray her character of an ethereal, supernatural being, but also highlighted her feet. Taglioni was the first to dance *en pointe* and this shorter-style skirt, although shocking at the time, was designed to show off her innovative footwork. These bell-shaped skirts can be seen in the paintings of Edgar Degas. The Italians shortened the skirt further during the 1870s to knee-length.

The increased popularity of pointe work meant a style of tutu began to evolve which was designed to frame the dancer's movements. Shorter and shorter skirts appeared, and in the 1940s wire hoops were first inserted into channels to enable the skirt to stand out from the hips and create the silhouette most people imagine today when they think of a plate tutu. The fabric for the skirts was originally stiffened tarlatan, then tulle and finally nylon net, which is still in current use.

Barbara Karinska was a Russian-born émigré who moved to New York and gained fame designing and making costumes. Working together with George Balanchine, she formulated a tutu which would not bob and dip, accommodating the fast-paced American style of ballet. Her tutu was shorter and tacked together loosely to create a softer look. It was originally designed for the ballet *Symphony in C* in 1950 and the popular style, which was copied all over the world, came to be known as a 'powder puff' tutu.

Ballet costume today is influenced to an extent by the fashions of the day. Indeed, several fashion designers, including Christian Lacroix, Karl Lagerfeld for Chanel, Jasper Conran and Isaac Mizrahi, have designed for the ballet.

The decoration, in this case the bodice embellishment, is sewn onto a net base.

A final note for those new to the craft of tutu-making

It is important to stress that there is no right way to make a tutu – I am constantly learning better or more efficient ways to do things, often thanks to my students. You may find other methods as you go along, so please change them to suit your needs, but I encourage you not to stray too far from the techniques here until you become familiar with them. It is important to stress the need to make everything robust, as a tutu is a costume which will undergo many demands in performance. It should be designed to be comfortable, to be worn without impeding the choreography and to be seen from a distance, with emphasis on this and not how it looks close up.

I teach a wide range of students – some need extra encouragement to be accurate and neat; others fuss over the tiniest mistake. You will have some idea which category you fit into. You should always aim to make everything beautifully, but as a general rule, if you have made an error, ask yourself if it will show on stage. If the answer is yes, then address the problem; if it will not be noticed in the stalls, stop fretting.

If tutu-making is new to you, even if your aim is to make a larger or adult size, I would recommend you start with the child's plate as you get a quicker result, will learn all the techniques, get some idea if it is within your abilities and, of course, make a child very happy.

CHAPTER 1

Fabrics and Equipment

Making a tutu is a complex project for a beginner. The correct fabrics and haberdashery will help you to achieve a good-quality result and the correct equipment will add to your efficiency. This chapter details the fabrics you will need to make the tutu, the haberdashery required, and finally a list of essential and desirable equipment to complete the garment.

Fabrics

The toile

You will need fabric from which to make a toile. This is a mock-up of the basic bodice and basque pattern in an inexpensive fabric to ensure it fits before cutting into more expensive fabrics. Creating an accurate pattern will also allow you to calculate more precisely the required quantity of fabric. Traditionally a toile would be made from calico, an unbleached cheap cotton which comes in various weights. A medium-weight calico would be ideal, but it is not necessary to buy something specially; similar cotton fabric left over from other projects or even an old sheet could be used.

Examples of calico, an inexpensive fabric used to make a toile.

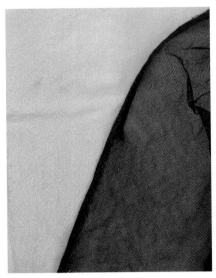

Cotton bobbinet, a high-quality woven net used to carry the net layers.

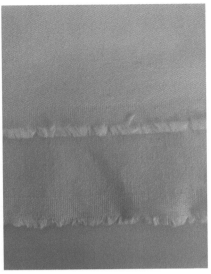

Cotton drill, used to make the basque and as a backing to add body to the bodice.

Tutu nets, available in many stiffness ratings and colours.

The tutu plate

Knicker

Cotton bobbinet is used to make the knicker. This is a high-quality woven net fabric which is strong and light, and is used in a double layer to carry the nets. Bobbinet, developed in the nineteenth century, was often used as a base to make corselettes for couture dresses. If you look inside a Dior ballgown, this durable, fine fabric is used as the base onto which the gown is stitched. Although it doesn't have stretch as such, it certainly has ease in one direction. When cutting the knicker out, this ease will go horizontally around the body, which will help the dancer to get into the costume and provide a little give for a larger size. Bobbinet is available in white, off-white and black, so you may decide to dye it if you are making a coloured tutu. Instructions for dyeing cotton bobbinet can be found in Chapter 8.

Nylon bobbinet is also available. It is cheaper than cotton bobbinet, but much less easy to use: when using it folded double, the layers slip against each other. I would always favour cotton bobbinet as it is stronger and easy to launder.

You may think Lycra would be a good choice for the knicker. However, it should not be used for a professional costume as it will perish over time and the tutu will not have longevity. I have worked on productions where the tutus are still being used 20 years after they were first made. However, you may decide that Lycra suits your purposes; if that is the case, I would recommend using it in a single layer.

Basque

The basque is best made from a good-quality fine cotton drill. White should suit most costumes, but you may prefer to use black if you are making a black or dark-coloured tutu. The style of bodice in this book is cut through the waist and finishes on the high hip line, completely covering the drill basque. If making for a child, a softer, finer cotton, like a cambric or sheeting with a plain weave, would be more suitable.

Tutu nets

Nylon net is used for the main part of the plate. The quality of net varies hugely, but I have suggested some suppliers at the end of the book. When I first started making tutus in the mid 1980s, very stiff net was available which made excellent, long-lasting tutus, but formaldehyde was used in the making process and concerns about its toxicity mean it is no longer available. There are alternative stiff nets on the market, which should be used for your tutu to have any kind of longevity.

For a professional tutu, I would use a combination of stiff and soft net. The stiff net is required to keep the shape of the tutu and the soft net is for added comfort – not only because the stiff net can be scratchy on the tutu wearer's legs, but also really disagreeable to their partner, especially in lifts. The leg ruffles should always be made from softer net to avoid them being uncomfortable. Due to the depth of an adult tutu, the stiffness rating for a professional tutu should be 40 or higher: failure to use this grade could result in a floppy plate. The stiffness rating for soft net should be around 10, or use a net like baroness tulle.

Some of the suppliers listed at the end of the book tend to work with professional companies and it may be difficult to buy smaller quantities of net from them. It is perfectly possible to make a tutu from net in your local fabric shop, but it is unlikely to stand up to the rigours of prolonged performance. It could work for a young dancer performing short pieces and who is likely to grow quickly, rather than for a tutu for a professional company that is likely to be worn by numerous dancers and to be in the repertoire for over twenty years. Use your judgement to decide which quality of net suits the requirement of your project.

I have never had much success dyeing net. It tends to crumple and it is not possible to get strong colours. Nylon net can be professionally dyed, but be warned that it can lose some of its substance in the process, so purchase it in the desired colour if possible.

The bodice

There are a huge range of textiles that would be suitable for the bodice top fabric. I would recommend a natural fibre like silk or cotton. A dupion or plain weave are especially suitable, but brocades work too. Be aware if your fabric has an obvious design as you may need to buy extra to pattern-match at the seams. If making for a professional dancer, be mindful that any dance partner will be in contact with the fabric, so it is important that it is not slippery, scratchy, beaded or heavily embellished around areas like the waist.

The bodice fabric will be backed with a cotton fabric like the drill used for the basque or similar. This will add strength and body to the costume. It is not necessary to colour-match this to the top fabric: white is fine, or you could use black if the bodice is dark. As for the basque, a finer cotton backing would work better for a child's costume.

A word on stretch fabrics. Professional dancers are used to rehearsing in comfortable ballet wear, and although for a professional costume I am not generally asked to use stretch fabric for the main part of the bodice, it is possible to cut a discreet panel like the side back from a stretch fabric. This shouldn't show in the finished bodice but will allow the dancer not to feel too constricted. Use a stretch fabric like a dense satin-backed Lycra, then back it with a conventional nylon Lycra. Sometimes a colour-matched conventional Lycra works well; this will have a shiny side and a matt side, so use the side that matches the top fabric best. If you are working for one of the big ballet companies and they have a printing and dyeing department, it may be possible to use digital printing techniques to copy any design on the main bodice fabric onto the panel fabric.

Sleeve fabric

Depending on the style and design of the sleeve these could be made from the bodice fabric, a soft net or something more diaphanous like chiffon.

Examples of silk dupion bodice fabrics.

Examples of delicate net fabrics suitable for sleeves and decoration.

Minx net, matched to the skin tone of the dancer and used to discreetly add structure to the bodice, for instance to fill in low necklines.

Illusion/minx net/souffle

This fabric is used as a flesh-toned infill, generally for a 'V' shape on a low bodice centre front or to extend a bodice neckline. It is generally used in a double layer and can provide modesty, comfort and security for the dancer. It should not show when on stage but blend in with the dancer's skin tone.

Shrinkage

The fabrics should be pre-washed before the garment is cut out as some textiles will contract by up to 15 per cent when laundered. Wash any fabric that could shrink: the drill backing, bodice fabric and knicker net. Nylon tutu net will not shrink so does not need pre-washing, but the rest of the costume is likely to get sweaty in wear and will need laundering at some point. It is therefore important not to skip this stage; it would be terrible to put so much work into finishing a garment to find it no longer fits after cleaning.

You will need to wash the bodice fabric, even if the manufacturer recommends dry-cleaning. You could hand wash it if it is especially delicate.

Any fancy fabrics containing a metal thread should also be steamed with a steam iron; they can shrink dramatically and it is vital that they contract now rather than under the iron after the garment has been cut out.

Haberdashery

Here are the essential items of haberdashery you should have to hand.

Polyester thread – Coats Astra 120, Gutermann Mara 120 or similar for machine stitching. Choose colours to match both the tutu net and bodice fabric if they are different. If your machine is able to wind a bobbin while sewing, two reels will be useful. This should be used to machine the bodice especially if it is made from stretch fabric.

Cotton thread – Coats Tre Cerchi or similar that is primarily used for hand-sewing. Some people prefer to stitch the bodice together with cotton thread, especially if the bodice is made of a natural fibre. You will need thread which matches the bodice, the tutu, stringing and decoration.

Contrast thread for tacking – any contrast-coloured cotton thread you have in your kit.

25mm-wide millinery Petersham ribbon – this is used for the tutu waistband and is generally white in colour, but use black if you are making a black or dark tutu. Steam to shrink before use.

25mm-wide elastic for the waistband – white or black to match the waistband fabric. Wash or steam to shrink before use.

12mm elastic for shoulder straps – get high-quality elastic, either in a skin tone, or use white and dye it yourself either with a cold-water dye or teabags and hot water. Alternatively, the dancer can cover the straps with their own foundation, a process known as 'pancaking', which will create a more accurate skin tone match. Wash or steam to shrink before use.

5mm elastic for the knicker legs – either in white, flesh tone or black. Wash or steam to shrink before use.

Corset hooks and bars – these large hooks will keep the waistband closed.

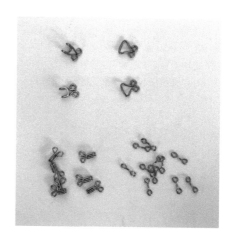

The upper image shows corset hooks, which are used on the waistband. The lower image shows size 3 hooks and bars.

Elastic shoulder straps can be dyed using cold-water dyes or dipped into a pot of tea. The longer they are left in the tea, the deeper the skin tone that can be achieved.

Size 3 dress hooks and bars – these are small fastenings which close the centre back of the bodice. Although the hooks are easy to buy in either a nickel finish or black-coated brass, the bar or loop element is increasingly hard to purchase as manufacturers have replaced them with eyes. There is a list of stockists at the back of the book, or you could ask older relatives who may have a stash not realising their value. The metal fastenings are essential for a professional costume, but a bar made from thread covered with buttonhole stitch or a chain stitch could work for a non-professional costume.

12mm cotton bias binding – white or black for the bottom of the basque and matching the colour of the knicker, or flesh-coloured for the knicker legs.

Narrow ribbon for hanging tapes – this can be India tape, ribbon or similar.

Size 00 cotton piping cord – this fine piping cord is the perfect scale for a costume. It is used to finish the top and bottom edges of the bodice and for decoratively piped seams. Pre-shrink it before use by washing it in hot water.

7mm plastic-covered or cotton-covered steel boning – this is used for the tutu hoop on a professional costume and is easily cut by folding it over and snapping the fold with pressure from pliers.
Or:
7mm plastic boning – this can also be used for the tutu hoop and would be suitable for a child or young adult's costume. It can be cut with paper or kitchen scissors. Occasionally, I have used both types of boning in the

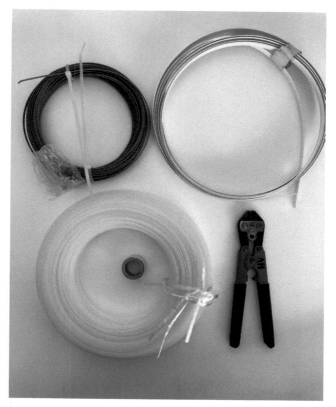

Examples of spiral boning used for the bodice, steel boning and plastic boning used for the tutu plate hoop. Pliers are needed to snip through the spiral boning.

channel – the plastic boning seems to stop the metal from bending out of shape so readily which is especially useful if there is a lot of partnering in the choreography.

7mm spiral boning – the bodice does not generally need boning, but if the centre front needs a bone to stay taught, or the dancer has a large bust, spiral boning will provide strength and flexibility. Spiral corset boning is made from two coils of steel wire that are flattened together. It is available already cut to length, or you may need to cut it using wire cutters. As it is constructed with two filaments of wire, it is easier to snip through each one separately rather than attempting to cut straight across. If left with a sharp, pointed edge, snip again closer to the core of the bone and then finish the ends. This should be done with the equivalent-size metal bone cap and two pairs of pliers, one of which should be dolphin-nosed – a pair of tweezers may suffice. Slot the cap onto the end of the bone and clamp in place, then use the pliers to clamp down the cap. This may need several attempts, but if it is correctly in place, it should be quite secure.

Zinc oxide tape – to close the tutu hoop.

Equipment

Here is a list of essential basic equipment followed by a list of desirable items which will help in creating a professional result.

Basic equipment

Sewing machine – you will need a domestic sewing machine with a swing needle: that is, one which is capable of stitching both a straight stitch and a zigzag stitch. These stitches will need to be easily adjustable in both length and width. It is quite likely that your machine has many further stitch options, but you will not need them for this project. My personal favourite machine is a Swiss-made Bernina. It has a metal casing, which means it has a good overall weight and will not shift about on the table like many modern machines. It also has an easily detachable table and the added advantage that the needle can be moved into five different positions. Although you can make a costume on an industrial machine, it is less easy to control when pleating the nets and it is an advantage for certain processes to use the free arm you get on a domestic machine.

Sewing machine needles – you will need a good supply of regular machine needles: a standard size 12 or 80 should be suitable for most of the fabrics you will use.

Sewing machine zipper foot – you will need a regular foot for most of the project. A zipper foot is useful for making the piping.

Dressmaking shears – these should only be used for cutting fabrics. They should have blades which are around 25cm long. There are many different makes available, but they don't need to be expensive. Some manufacturers also offer a scissor sharpener, which is useful for keeping the cutting edge honed.

Paper scissors – these are used for pattern-making and cutting the net edges. Net can blunt scissors, especially when cutting several layers of net at once.

Small embroidery scissors – these are used at the sewing machine for cutting threads and for hand-sewing.

Dressmaking pins – these are used for pinning the paper pattern onto the fabrics and for pinning the costume together in preparation for sewing the fabric pieces together. Fine, long nickel pins are most suitable as they will glide easily through the fabric.

Glass or plastic-headed pins – these are used for the tutu; once the plate begins to take shape, ordinary dressmaking pins become very difficult to see in the pleated nets. The coloured heads of these pins make them much easier to spot.

Safety pins of various sizes – you should have a good number of medium-sized safety pins for general use and fittings, small ones to feed the leg elastics through the knicker leg, and a large one to aid feeding the hoop through the net channel.

Tape measure – the ideal measure has both metric and imperial measurements on both sides. Each unit has its merits and I often switch between the two depending on the process I am carrying out.

Pencil – I favour a mechanical pencil, which is especially useful when pattern-drafting. However, a conventional HB pencil is good to draft with and you will need a softer one if you use it to mark the net edges. These pencils will need regular sharpening.

White chalk pencil – this is useful for marking dark fabrics.

Vanishing fabric marker – these felt-tip pens mark textiles and then vanish over time and are available from specialist suppliers. Always test on the fabric you are using as they last varying lengths of time and they may vanish too quickly for your use. Friction pens are available from conventional stationers, and come in a variety of colours. They can be erased from fabric with steam, but again test on the fabric before using them, as they have a hard tip and can damage delicate textiles.

Examples of fabric markers including mechanical pencils, friction pens and a vanishing fabric marker pen.

Dressmaker's tracing wheels with differing profiles. The pointed wheels work well on drill; the wheels with a smoother edge work well on the knicker net.

Ruler – this is used to draft patterns. A 30cm plastic ruler is best, and the specialist pattern-making version, which is flexible and inscribed with horizontal marks to aid with marking seam allowances, is ideal.

Metre rule – this is used to mark out the net in preparation for cutting out.

Dressmaker's carbon paper – one of the big differences between fashion/home dressmaking and costume-making is the seam allowances. In costume-making we need to make sure we can alter a costume to fit a different or growing performer. To this end different-sized seam allowances are marked throughout the garment, but the original pattern shape needs to be marked with waxy carbon paper. It is made by several manufacturers, but I favour the one made by Burda. I like to use the yellow paper on a white garment as it is discreet but still visible.

Dressmaker's tracing wheels – these are the tools that, combined with carbon paper, enable you to transfer the paper pattern to the cloth. Ideally, you will need one with sharp needle-points and one with a smoother edge; you can then select the most suitable for the job at hand – often one will work better than the other.

Pattern paper or brown paper – spot and cross paper is used by pattern drafters. It is not essential, but the grid markings aid swift pattern creation.

Masking or Magic Tape – sticky tape which you are able to write over is useful for pattern-drafting.

Iron – most domestic steam irons will also have a function that enables you to direct steam. This will be needed when we come to set the plate into shape.

Dressmaker's carbon paper is available in many different qualities and colours. Choose a contrast colour which will show up on your fabric.

Ironing board – a conventional ironing board with a cotton cover will suffice; a large, flat ironing table would be a luxury.

Fabric weights or full tin cans – weights are used in place of pins wherever possible while cutting out the nets. Although fabric weights are available to buy, you can use anything heavy. I like full tin cans; they do the job just as well.

Hand-sewing needles – I favour No. 9 sharps for hand-sewing and longer needles like saddlers or upholstery needles are useful for stringing the nets together.

Thimble – always use a thimble when hand-sewing. Many of the techniques we will use require stitching through several layers of fabric at once, so a thimble is essential. I prefer a tailor's thimble, which has an open top.

Pin cushion – this is used to keep all the needles in one place. The prickly net edges of a tutu have a habit of picking up loose threads, so getting into the habit of using a pin cushion means you will never lose your needles.

Calculator – this is used to calculate many of the complex sums associated with altering patterns and fabric quantities.

Other desirable equipment

Overlocker – an overlocker is a machine which neatly cuts a seam allowance and then stitches over the edge to prevent fraying in one process. If you are thinking of investing in an overlocker, consider what you will use it for; a three-thread overlocker is sufficient for this tutu project, but if you are likely to use it for stretch wear such as leotards, a four-thread machine would be better. Some overlockers can also be adapted to create a small turned edge which can be used to finish bias hems. Although overlockers are useful and efficient, a similar effect can be created with a sewing machine by running a straight stitch close to the edge of the seam allowance, cutting this back neatly and then zigzagging with the needle on the left, entering the fabric to the left of the stitched edge with the right side of the zigzag stitching

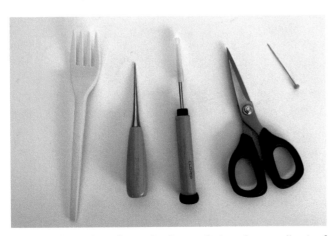

Tools used to aid machine-pleating – a fork, awls, a small pair of embroidery scissors and a large, glass-headed pin.

going over the straight stitch and the raw edge. This is more time-consuming but perfectly serviceable if you don't wish to invest in an overlocker.

Sewing machine buttonhole foot – a buttonhole foot is useful for creating buttonholes and stitching piping onto the bodice.

Sleeve board – this is a mini-ironing board and is useful for pressing small areas of the costume which are tricky to press on a full board because of their size and location.

Tailoring hams – these are useful for pressing the curved seams on the bodice. They come in various sizes and although available to buy, they can be quite expensive. They are easy enough to make yourself – one side should be cotton, the other side a woollen fabric – and they are traditionally stuffed with sawdust.

Wooden-handled awl – this is helpful when pleating up the nets. These will be hand-folded as you machine them together, and although a pin or small pair of scissors can be used, an awl sits nicely in the hand and offers good manoeuvrability.

Beeswax – this is used to aid hand-sewing. It is particularly useful when joining the basque to the knicker as it helps the thread to pass smoothly through all the layers and makes it less likely to shear off at the eye of the needle.

French curve – this is a plastic template used to refine the curves while drafting patterns.

'L' square – this is useful for squaring off the net fabric while cutting out the tutu layers.

Mannequin – a high-quality linen-covered dress mannequin with legs is useful for draping your own patterns and steaming the tutu plate. These are a big investment, so unless you are setting up a business, it is not necessary to have one. It is possible to use a tailor's dummy made from jersey-covered high-impact polystyrene which is easily available and useful for checking the bodice, but unless it has legs it will not be possible to check the plate. A child's shop mannequin can be a good investment if you are considering making a set of costumes for children. For adults, it is easier to pad up a small dummy with wadding to the required size than use a dummy which is larger than your needs. When constructing a made-to-measure garment, I will often do this.

Pliers – if using steel boning, use pliers to cut the bones and an additional pair of dolphin-nosed pliers to aid in attaching the caps.

Labels – a professional company may have their own labels where details like the dancer's name and character can be added. You could also consider using your own labels if you are going into costume-making as a career.

Pinking shears – these are useful for producing a decorative finish.

Measurements

When making a costume for a client, it is important to have accurate measurements. Try to take these yourself if possible, and measure over close-fitting clothing like a leotard. It is useful to have a mirror in the room to check the tape is level around the body, and handy also to have a second person to take notes and read out the measurements.

The basic measurements you will need for this project are: height, chest, waist, high hip, hip, nape to waist, half girth and the distance between waist and hip.

Other measurements to add to your chart could include: head, neck, wrist, waist to floor (side), full girth, upper arm. Choose the ones that you think would be useful for your design.

Other useful information could include any allergies (some people are allergic to latex, washing powders or certain fabrics), bra size, shoe size, tights size, glove size, hair colour, if the dancer's ears are pierced, and so on. Just adapt the chart for your own situation.

The natural waist is the smallest part of the torso, just above the navel. This becomes more defined in young teenagers. Tie a length of elastic around the natural waist to have a consistent measuring point when taking the nape to waist and the girth measurements, or if you

Tip

You may find it useful to make a Word template – I keep one as a document on my computer and it is useful to reference if you make costumes regularly for the same dancer.

If you are making costumes for a corps or set of costumes, it is helpful to make a single chart as you can input the data and then rearrange the dancers into size order.

Use a measurement chart like the example given here. Start by writing the dancer's name at the top of the sheet, and date it.

Measurement Chart

An example of a measurement chart for recording the basic measurements needed for a tutu. Adapt it to your own needs.

Name

Date

Height

Chest

Waist

High hip

Hip

Nape to waist

Waist to hip

Half girth

Upper arm

Head

Neck

Wrist

Full girth

Waist to floor

Bra size

Shoe size

Glove size

Tights size

Allergies

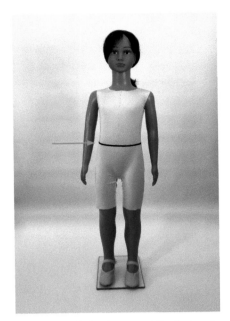

Tie a piece of elastic around the 'natural' or smallest part of the waist.

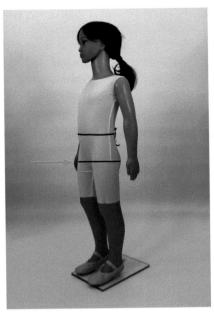

The hip measurement should be taken around the widest part of the bottom.

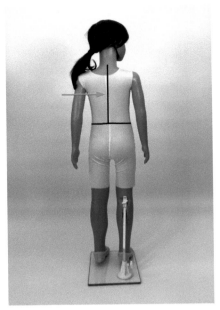

The nape to waist measurement is taken from the bone at the base of the neck to the waist.

are going to measure several dancers, stitch a button onto a length of buttonhole elastic so you do not have to knot it each time. This elastic belt gives you a consistent measuring point when taking the vertical measurements. Some dancers are surprised at how high the waist measurement is as most modern clothing has a lower waistline, but the waistband on a tutu should sit on the natural waist.

The high hip is 5cm below the waist for a child, 6.25cm for a teen, and for an adult it would be 7.5cm. This is an important measurement, as this is where the tutu plate will begin and where the bodice ends.

The hip is the widest part of the bottom half of the body. Set the tape measure in place and then check from the side that you have the correct position.

The distance from the waist to the hip, taken at the side, is useful for checking the knicker pattern.

The nape to waist measurement is taken at the back, from the prominent bone at the base of the neck to the bottom of the elastic around the waist at the centre back.

Because a child is likely to grow at speed, we will be constructing the costume to allow for some alteration.

The measurements used for the patterns in this book are shown in the chart below.

Pattern Measurements

Patterns are given in three sizes with the following measurements

	Metric			Imperial		
	Child	Teen	Adult	Child	Teen	Adult
Height	130cm	155cm	165cm	4ft 3in	5ft 1in	5ft 5in
Chest	56cm	71cm	86.5cm	22in	28in	34in
Waist	52cm	58.5cm	63.5cm	20½in	23in	25in
High hip	58.5cm	68.5cm	79cm	23in	27in	31in
Hip	61cm	76cm	91.5cm	24in	30in	36in
Waist to hip	11.5cm	15cm	20cm	4½in	6in	8in
Waist to high hip	7.5cm	6.25cm	5cm	3in	2½in	2in
Nape to waist	28cm	33cm	38cm	11in	13in	15in
Half girth	40.5cm	52.5cm	65cm	16in	20¾in	25½in
Top arm	18cm	22cm	25cm	7¼in	8¾in	10in

Glossary

CF – Centre Front, an imaginary line straight down the centre of the front of the body or a pattern piece that sits there.

SF – Side Front, a pattern piece, for instance in a bodice, which joins to the CF.

SSF – a Side Front pattern piece which is closer to the side seam than the SF. The teen and adult bodice patterns in this book have this additional pattern piece.

CB – Centre Back, an imaginary line, straight down the centre of the body at the back, or a pattern piece that sits there.

SB – Side Back, a pattern piece, for instance in a bodice, that joins the side seam to the CB.

SS – Side Seam, a seam positioned on the side of the body.

RS – Right Side (of the fabric), the side of the fabric you want to be visible in the finished costume.

WS – Wrong Side (of the fabric), the side of the fabric that faces the body when worn.

Edge stitch – a row of machine stitching, around 1 or 2mm from the edge.

Foots width – a row of stitching whereby you run the edge of the sewing machine foot along a specified line or edge of the garment in order to produce a stitch 5–6mm from the reference point.

Four-thread – four lengths of cotton thread folded over and used together for strength when hand-sewing.

Hand stitches

Although it is preferable to use the sewing machine for most of the processes in this book as its stitching provides speed and strength, there are occasions, particularly towards the completion of the tutu, where some hand-stitching will be required.

To fasten on, if using a single thread, make a small knot in the end and hide this in the seam allowance if possible. This is not only neat, but stops any possibility of discomfort for the dancer by the knot rubbing against their skin. If using a double thread, pass the two cut thread ends through the eye of the needle, creating a loop of thread. Take a small stitch and then pass the needle through the thread loop and pull the threads tight to create a neat, discreet fastening-on.

Fasten off with three small stitches sewn on top of each other, before cutting the remaining thread close to the final stitch.

A four-thread is regularly used for many processes in costume-making. It is a length of cotton thread, approximately 2.5m in length. Both cut ends are posted through the eye of a needle, and the cut ends aligned with the loop that is created, thus making four parallel threads of equal length. Tie all four threads together in a small, neat knot at the end. This creates a strong thread for sewing, and fewer stitches are needed, for instance when sewing on hooks and bars, than would be required with a single thread. Dance costumes are generally put under a lot of stress, so it is vital that they are robust and stand up to the rigours of the artform.

A good-quality cotton thread is necessary for sewing on fastenings by hand. Polyester thread will tend to knot as it has some stretch in it and will 'bounce' as you stitch,

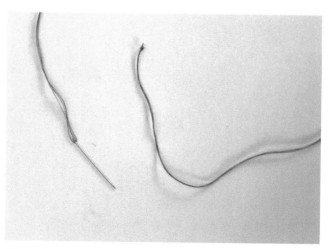

A four-thread.

Slip stitch.

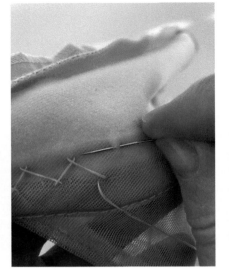

Herringbone stitch.

Stab stitch.

and makes it less easy to sew with speed. Cotton thread can still knot and shear through at the needle eye if the needle is regularly passing through several tough layers of fabric, but running the four-thread through some beeswax should help with these challenges.

Slip stitch

Slip stitch is used to discreetly catch back turnings. Use a double thread and fasten on. To catch back piping, for example, slip the needle through the piped edge fold about 1cm and then take a small stitch in the bodice backing which does not go through to the top fabric. This stitch should only take one or two warp threads from the fabric so it is as inconspicuous as possible on the right side. Repeat the process until the stitching is complete and fasten off.

Herringbone stitch

Herringbone stitch is commonly used to catch down turnings or hold the excess elastic from the shoulder straps in place. This stitch is generally done with a double cotton thread in a colour which will blend in with the garment. While executing herringbone stitch, the needle faces the opposite way to the direction of the stitch.

Stab stitch

Stab stitch is used with a four-thread to robustly anchor two crucial junctions of the costume. It is simply a large stitch which often gets hidden in the ditch of a piped edge and passes all the way through the costume from the front to the back. For example, to join the shoulder elastics to the bodice, layer three stitches on top of one another.

Back stitch.

Back stitch

Back stitch is used to firmly connect two elements of the costume. Fasten on and bring the needle to the right side through the layers which need connecting, take a small stitch of around 5mm in the reverse direction to that being stitched and stab back through the fabric. Take a larger stitch of about 1cm on the inside, before returning the needle to the top side and then repeating the process. In the example shown, on the top side small stitches of 5mm will be evident with 5mm gaps between; if connecting a piped edge, these stitches will sink into the ditch of the piping. The underside will show overlapping stitches. This stitch can be done with a double thread, but use a four-thread if the seam needs to be particularly robust, for example to stitch the tutu knicker to the basque.

CHAPTER 2

Getting Started

A design is usually created at the beginning of a project to give the interested parties an idea of the concept. There may be slight changes as the costume concept develops, but it is a good practice as a maker to have an idea of what is expected. You may be working with an established designer or a designer who has not worked in the dance world before and therefore needs guidance, or you may be thinking of designing the costume yourself.

There are three main design decisions that need to be made before making a tutu: the first is the shape and depth of the tutu plate. There are definite trends in tutu styles, often reflecting the fashion of the time. The two main tutu plate shapes are a pancake or drop tutu.

Pancake tutus stick out from the high hip and are strung to give a flat appearance like a dinner plate. The distance between the high hip and the edge of the top layer is known as the tutu depth. This depth depends to some extent on the look required, but in my experience this should not exceed 40cm, as that is the limit at which the hoop and net combined can realistically maintain the iconic flat shape. Examples of these tutus include the Royal Ballet's *Sleeping Beauty* Aurora tutus and those worn in *La Bayadere* by the dancers portraying the Shades in many productions around the world.

The top tutu has points which give it a more defined, sharp finish. The lower illustration shows a similar tutu but with scalloped edging.

The images show the front, side and back views of a pancake tutu plate. This is a traditional tutu plate and sticks out horizontally from the high hip.

The images show the front, side and back views of a drop tutu plate. This has a softer look than the pancake tutu.

These front, side and back images show variations on the basic pattern and how the effect can be varied by using different colours, with the addition of draped sleeves and with different decoration.

A drop tutu has a softer, more rounded bell shape. Again, the depth chosen for the deepest layer will depend on the design – a shorter tutu depth will have a different look to a deeper tutu depth, which is likely to look softer and more feminine. Examples of drop tutus include those used in the Mariinsky's *Paquita*, and the Royal Ballet's Sugar Plum Fairy costume, or the corps de ballet swan costumes in their 2018 production of *Swan Lake*.

The powder puff tutu was originated by Karinska and Balanchine in the 1950s. They are similar to the tutu plates in this book having a short net skirt, but are fluffier, have fewer layers and no hoop, and are strung quite loosely to give a softer overall look. Examples include the costumes for the original NYCB production of *Symphony in C*.

The depth of the top layer of the tutu will be dictated partly by the design and partly by the height of the dancer. A petite dancer can look swamped in a tutu which is too deep, and conversely a taller dancer in a too-short tutu will look out of balance. If making for a corps or a set for similar-sized dancers, the depth of the top layer of the tutu may need to be adjusted according to the dancer's height in order for the proportions to look similar on stage. These adjustments are subtle but help give a unified look.

Decide on the shape of the finished edge. Would you prefer points or scallops? They give different effects with the scallops looking softer in comparison to the points. One of the prettiest tutus I made was for Maria Bjornson's 1994 production of *Sleeping Beauty* for the Royal Ballet. The points on those tutus were 50 per cent longer than usual and curled up to resemble chrysanthemums. You may, of course, wish to develop your own unique templates.

The second decision concerns the construction and style of the bodice. Although the bodice generally ends on the high hip line where it meets the tutu, choices about the neckline and sleeves need to be made before considering fabric choices. The neckline needs careful evaluation and should flatter the dancer. Any neckline seen in regular garments could be considered, but the higher the neckline the more difficult it is to execute well: the dancer's extension often means the front bodice needs to be long in order not to affect movement, but it also needs to look good when standing still. It is for this reason that the neckline generally finishes in a gentle curve or plunge at the CF with support from souffle and straps.

Piping can be used as a design feature by incorporating it into a seam, especially if it is in a contrast fabric. It will make the seam which contains it difficult to alter later, so be selective in the seams you choose to pipe.

Examples of various fabrics showing both their right and wrong sides. Using a combination of both sides of the fabric can be very effective.

This piping can be created in the bodice fabric or in a contrasting fabric.

Will the costume have sleeves? Included in the book are instructions for armband sleeves and draped sleeves. Armband sleeves are strips of fabric gathered with an elasticated channel which slip onto the arm; there can be a single band or a second band which makes a puff in the centre. A draped sleeve is a longer length of fabric which joins the bodice around the pitch point at the front and marries to the corresponding point on the back. These will need an additional elastic loop around the arm to ensure they return to the correct position after movement. Set in sleeves are possible, but tricky to get right as they must not impede the movement of the arm. They also tend not to be favoured by choreographers as they can distract from the movement of the arm.

Once the design decisions for the bodice and tutu plate have been made, fabric choices and colours can be considered. Will the tutu plate be one colour, or a mixture – do you want it to grade in colour as it moves from the lower net layers to the upper net layers?

Will the bodice be made of the same fabric throughout? Some fabrics have a reverse side which can be used to good effect, for instance on the bodice CF panel. The fabric should have some stability and strength, but there are really no rules as to colour choice or how many different fabrics the costume should contain. Be aware that pale colours can look washed-out under stage lighting, so don't be afraid to be bold with colour choice as subtlety doesn't always read well from a distance.

The third design decision is that of decoration. This is generally a separate entity which will enable easy alteration and may need to be removed for cleaning, so it needs careful consideration. Frequently, a top skirt is added to the top of the tutu plate, which may be made of

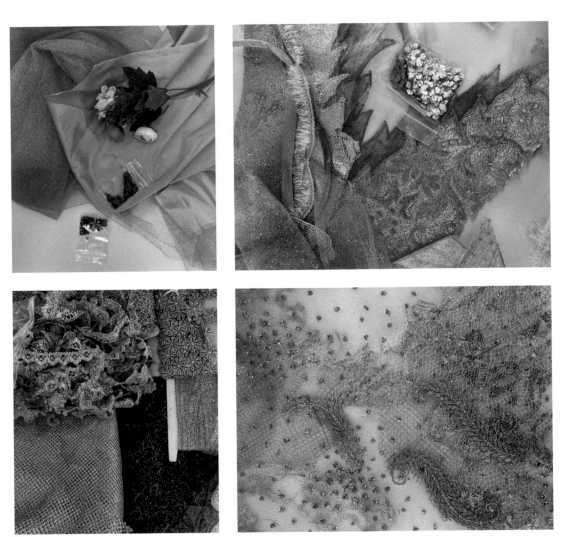

Gather together embellishments and other inspiration to try out ideas before deciding on a final design.

the same fabric as the bodice or a contrast net. This can be further embellished with other fabric, appliqué, trims or beading, but attention should be given to the weight as heavy decoration will affect the shape of the finished tutu plate. The decoration on the top skirt should either be random or finish accurately on the CF. Dancers are used to seeing their feet when they rehearse and use this to help centre themselves when pirouetting. It's therefore important they aren't put off-balance by unintended asymmetry in the decoration.

The CF panel is often decorated, although avoid heavy decoration around the waist if the dancer is to be partnered. Also be aware of how the bodice reacts to the dancer's movements and avoid placing too much decoration where it may be uncomfortable for the dancer, like under the arms.

Does the costume need additional accessories like a headdress or jewellery? Necklaces or the effect of one are generally stitched onto a flesh-coloured mesh which is then hooked onto the bodice, to avoid jewellery bouncing around in performance.

If you are not working with a costume designer, you will need to consider the design yourself before you start. The internet is a good resource where you can look up images of various professional companies' tutu designs or costumes suitable for competitions, depending on your requirements. However, great inspiration can be found in books, from old costumes, fashion magazines and art galleries, in researching costume history, or by looking at existing tutus. Start by collecting pictures you are inspired by and refer to them throughout the making process. Design decisions are often adapted as the costume evolves, but it is a good idea to sketch a design or have other images as a starting point.

It should always be remembered that the costume exists to enhance the performance and aid the characterisation, and not to distract from the dance, so think carefully about the proportion of the costume and the character you are trying to portray.

Copying the patterns

Included in this book are patterns to make a basque, knicker and bodice, together with tutu plate recipes, in three different sizes. They are created on spot and cross paper where each mark is on a 2.5cm/1in grid.

These sheets can be scaled up using similar squared paper, or use a photocopier to increase the scale. Compare the measurements of your dancer to those of the patterns and select the set which most closely resembles them not only in circumference but also the length of their body. If either of these differ significantly from the three sizes provided, now is the time to alter the pattern. This is most easily done by splicing the pattern piece where the amendment is required and then sticking it back together accommodating the alteration using Magic Tape or masking tape.

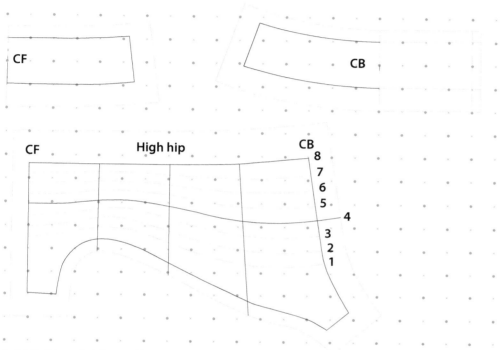

A child's 8-layer knicker and basque pattern.

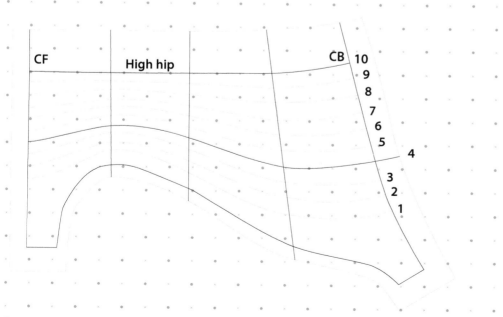

A teenager's 10-layer knicker pattern.

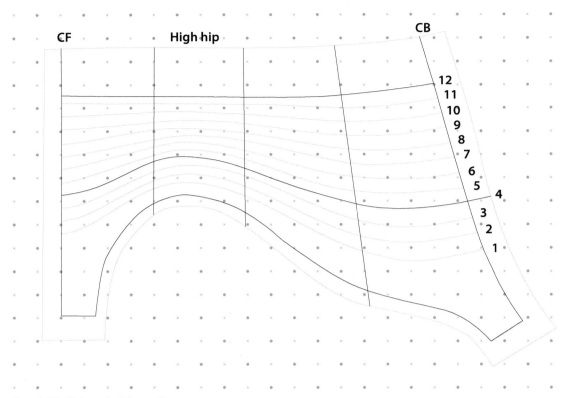

An adult's 12-layer knicker pattern.

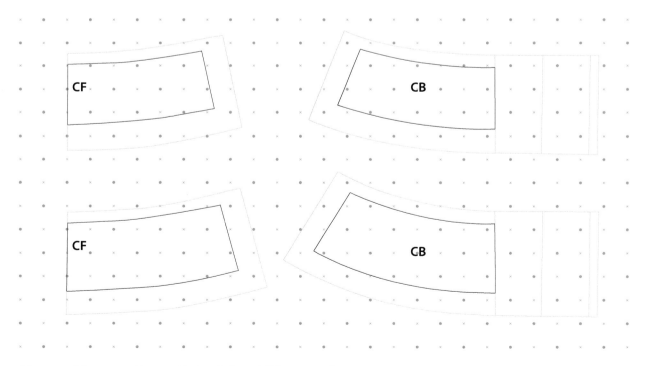

A teenager's basque pattern and below it, the adult basque pattern.

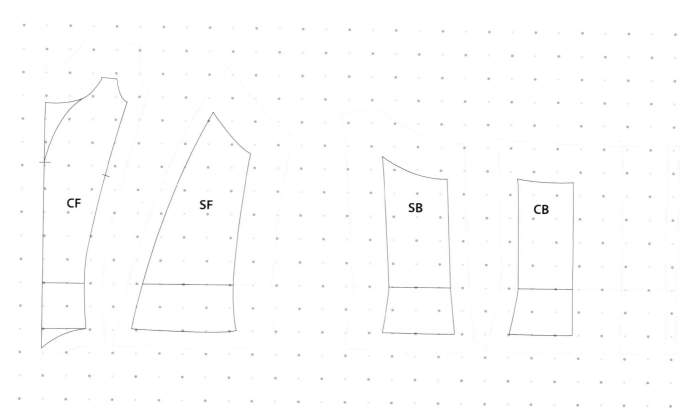

A child's 8-piece bodice pattern.

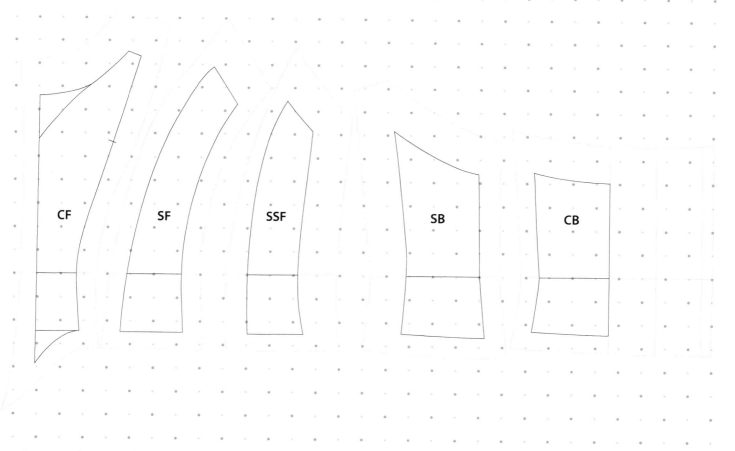

A teenager's 10-piece bodice pattern.

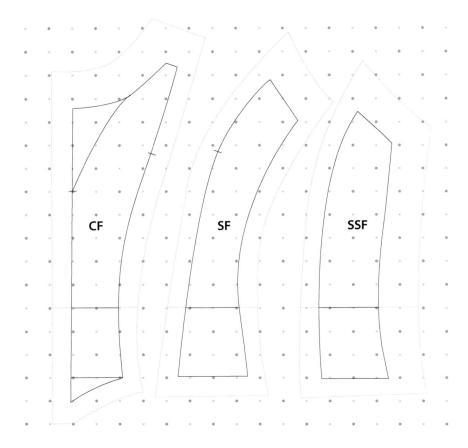

The front section of an adult's 10-piece bodice pattern.

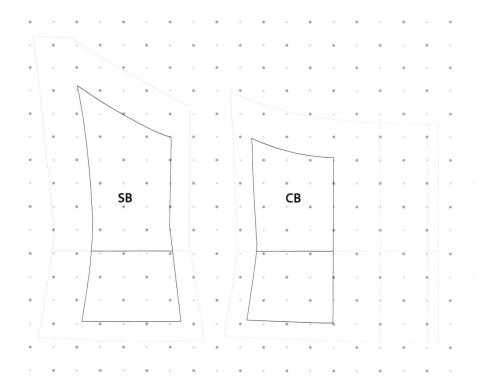

The back section of an adult's 10-piece bodice pattern.

Do remember that you will do a fitting, so a certain amount of alteration and refinement will still need to be done after the toile has been fitted on the dancer.

Most costume-makers will not add seam allowances to their patterns, but mark these straight onto the fabric, or even cut them by eye. The reason for this is that each pattern piece will be traced around using dressmaker's carbon paper and it is vital that this is done accurately. The diagrams have the seam allowances included so if you would rather create the pattern with these included, please do add them at this stage. Be aware that using a tracing wheel can damage the pattern, so think about this if you intend to use the pattern more than once.

You may prefer to use your own bodice pattern, in which case make sure the waist on the pattern is around 1.5cm bigger than the waist measurement to allow enough ease for it to sit over the tutu waistband.

Making a calico toile

Making a toile is extremely useful in helping to establish an accurate pattern and I would strongly recommend making one. This simple mock-up tests the precision of your pattern in inexpensive fabric, reducing waste before committing to cut into the more expensive top fabrics. It also means there are likely to be fewer alterations in the final garment, which helps to keep the costume looking fresh and clean.

The toile can be kept as a record for future projects with notes highlighting any issues you would address for subsequent orders.

Cutting out the calico toile

Fold the calico in half along the lengthwise grain, matching the selvedges. Keeping the grainline true is vital to achieving a good-quality result. In the case of the bodice, we need to keep the waistline running at 90 degrees to the lengthwise grain. The CF and CB of the basque need to sit vertically along the warp of the fabric. If you have opted to go for a bodice without a CF seam, place this piece on the fold of the calico first and fit all the other pieces around it, using the fabric as economically as possible.

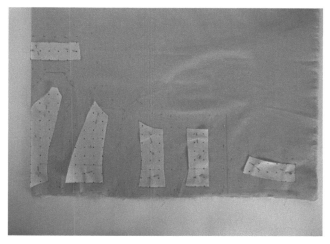

Cut out the calico toile as economically as possible.

Dressmaker's carbon paper will be used to accurately mark the lines, so bear this in mind when pinning out the pattern. The calico is 'sticky' enough to require only a very little pinning – two pins per pattern piece should be enough on pieces this size – and be aware to keep the pins away from the trace lines. You will need to mark the seam allowances onto the cloth in pencil – if you feel confident, you can do this by eye. For the bodice, allow 5cm on the CB, 4cm on the side seams and the top or neckline edge, 2.5cm on the bottom edge and 2cm on the remaining bodice seams. On the basque, allow 1.5cm above the waist, 2.5cm below the high hip, 4cm on the side seams and 5cm beyond the CB line. When you are happy with how all the pattern pieces are laid out, and the seam allowances are marked, cut out the toile using dressmaker's scissors. Although not essential, it is a good habit to leave a triangle of fabric on any CFs, as even if they are removed later, they are a useful pointer to the exact CF on a piece of fabric.

Some makers like to cut the SF panel on the bias, and although it initially provides a good fit, it can stretch and distort in wear.

Dancers are used to comfortable Lycra practice clothing and you could cut the SB panel from stretch fabric so the garment feels less structured. A satin Lycra dyed to match the top fabric and used either shiny or matt side out, depending on which is the most discreet, and with the stretch going around the body would provide some comfort. If you decide to do this, stitch a vertical pleat into the calico pattern to remove one eighth of its width. The satin Lycra should be backed flat onto ordinary nylon Lycra and machine-tacked in place; the process of mounting fabric pieces together will be dealt with in detail in Chapter 4, but in this case, as the fabric stretches, use a zigzag stitch for the machine tack so it doesn't constrict the pattern piece or snap during wear.

Although it is important to be accurate, remember you should have the advantage of two fittings, so it is easier to adapt the shape on the dancer than spend time making the toile fit the measurements exactly as they may have changed since they were taken.

Marking out fabrics

Costume-makers use dressmaker's carbon paper. This is different to fashion industry or home dressmaking patterns which have standard 15mm or ⅝in seam allowances. It enables you to have different seam allowance widths for different seams, which can be very useful for alterations.

Cut a piece of dressmaker's carbon paper that is about A4 in size and fold it down the length to make a long strip with the waxy side on the outside. The tracing wheel can sometimes damage the table it is used on, so protect any precious surfaces with a cutting board or piece of cardboard. Test the fabric to ensure the carbon leaves a clear mark. If you have a choice of tracing wheels, test them all before deciding which results in the best trace line without damaging the fabric.

When you are happy with your test results, take a cut section of the calico toile and carefully peel back the pattern and top piece of calico. Insert the dressmaker's carbon paper between the two pieces of fabric. Pat the sandwich down flat, ensuring it is sitting neatly and the underneath layer is not rumpled.

Accurately trace the outer pattern lines and any construction lines like the waistline with firm, sweeping strokes from the wheel, going into the seam allowances from raw edge to raw edge to aid accurate assembly. Wherever there is an acute angle, like at the top of the CB section where it will join the SB section, mark an additional dash which will help smooth out any inaccuracies in the tracing process.

It is unlikely any of these pattern pieces will become confused, but you can label them with pencilled initials like CF/SF/SSF/SB/CB in the seam allowance. I would also label them with the dancer's initials in the event I was making a set of costumes. Unpin the pattern from the calico in preparation for machine thread-marking.

Thread up the sewing machine with contrasting thread – this is a good opportunity to use up unused thread on bobbins from previous projects. Any colour will work as long as it is a good contrast as you will need to see the lines during the fitting. Use a long stitch length and stitch the following lines directly on top of the traced mark.

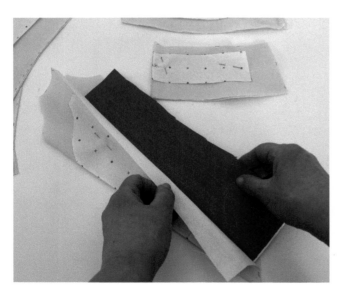

Insert the folded dressmaker's carbon paper into the middle of the cut-out pattern pieces and pat down flat.

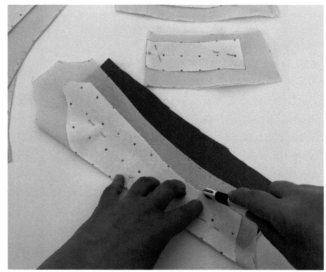

Use a dressmaker's tracing wheel to accurately trace the edge of the pattern. Use the fingers of your free hand to stop the pattern shifting.

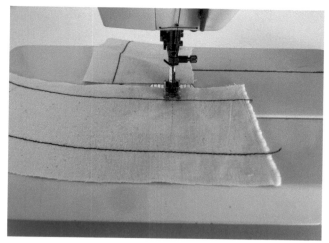

Machine thread-mark exactly on the marked lines in a contrasting thread. These important markings will be clearly visible in the fitting.

- On the basque, the waistlines, high hip, CF and CBs.
- On the bodice, the waistlines, high hip, lower edge if it comes away at the CF to a point, CB and neck or top line.

Stitch each of these directly on top of the marked line from raw edge to raw edge; try to get into the habit of sewing across several pieces in one process, then cutting them apart afterwards, as you if making bunting. This will help with speed and also save thread.

Assembling the toile

Pin together the bodice sections in pairs; the CB to SB, SB to SF, SF to CF and so on for the child and teen size. The adult pattern has an additional bust seam, so pin together the CFs, SF to SSF, and SB to CB. Also pin together the side seams on the basque. All the seams should fit perfectly together with no bubbling. If there is any discrepancy, assume the waistline is correct and place the excess above or below this line. Machine together using a long stitch, beginning at the raw edge and adding a small reverse stitch within the pattern area of the bodice or basque to avoid the stitching unravelling. Then pin and stitch together the side seams on the bodice. You can press these if you want, but often 'finger pressing' (running your nail along the seam) should be sufficient: using this technique also means the seam retains a softness that is lost when pressed open with an iron. Use a safety pin to attach the shoulder straps, leaving a 2.5cm seam allowance on the front section, and 7.5cm on the back, which can be pinned to the outside to allow for easy alteration.

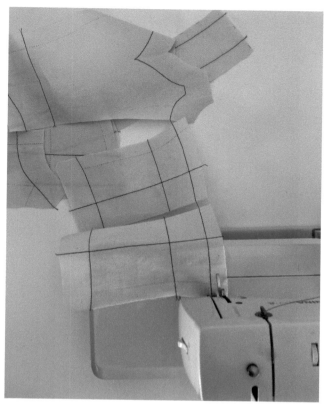

For efficiency, sew across several pieces at once, cutting them apart afterwards.

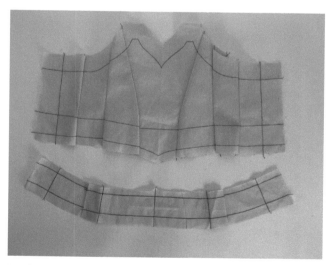

Machine-stitch the bodice and basque together.

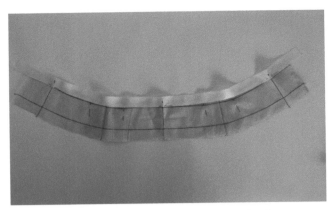

Pin the Petersham ribbon waistband to the inside of the basque.

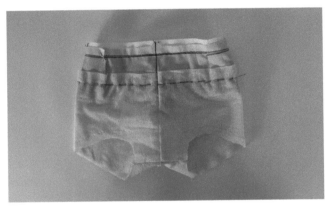

If desired, the knicker can be fitted at the first fitting. Pin and then tack it together at the high hip line.

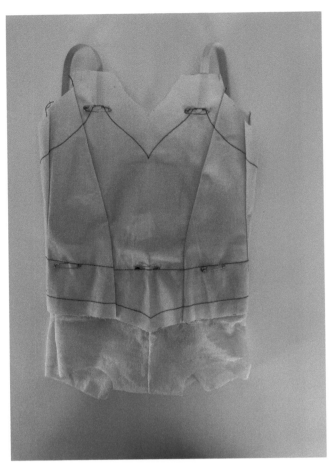

Attach the waist of the bodice to the waist of the basque underneath the waistband using safety pins.

To make the basque, take the 2.5cm-wide Petersham ribbon and cut a piece as long as the dancer's waist measurement plus 20cm. Put a small pencil dot at the centre of the ribbon. Then divide the waist measurement in half and mark this distance from the CF dot to indicate the position of the CBs. Match one edge of the Petersham to the marked waistline on the side of the basque without seam allowances, starting at the raw edges, and ensuring the CB and CF dots on the Petersham waistband correspond with the CB and CF lines on the basque. Use a long stitch for this as it will be removed after the fitting.

To get an exact girth measurement which will aid drafting an accurate knicker pattern, attach a length of ribbon or tape to the outside of the high hip line at the CF with a safety pin. This will be taken through the dancer's legs to the CB hip line and pinned during the fitting; allow about 45cm for a child, 55cm for a teen and 65cm for an adult.

You can decide whether to fit the knicker at this stage, before it is attached to the net, as there are pros and cons. One advantage is that you can see if the dancer needs an adjusted leg line and that the girth and general fit is good. Fitting the knicker at this stage also presents

an opportunity to get an accurate measurement of the hip where the channel layer will sit, which will provide a reference point for the length of the hoop. The disadvantage is that the knicker style is not very flattering, and the focus of the person being fitted is often directed to this aspect of the costume. The knicker disappears under the net in a completed tutu, so the problem disappears, too.

If your preference is to fit the knicker before it is attached to the net, follow the instructions in Chapter 3: 'Making the knicker' without marking each of the net layer lines at this stage in case their position changes – just mark the essential bold lines on the pattern. Stop before the instructions for 'Making the CB opening'. Cut the knicker sections out with plenty of seam allowance so the fabric is there if it needs alteration after fitting. Hand-tack the CB from the crotch to the CB opening and then tack the crotch seam, but not all the way through the seam allowances as this will tighten the leg and distort the fit. With the allowances on the inside, hand-tack the high hip line of the knicker to the high hip on the basque matching the CBs, CFs and side seams. The high hip should have a little excess in the knicker; it should certainly not be stretched onto the basque.

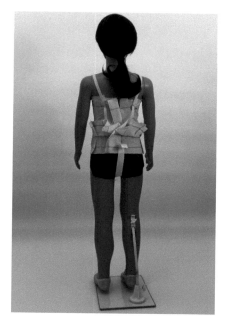

Pin down the CB of the basque at the point where it fits smoothly. Then pin the crotch tape to the CB high hip point.

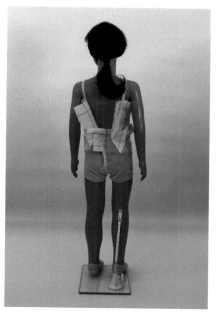

If fitting the knicker, check the fit at the back: it shouldn't be tight over the bottom. At this stage the knicker leg turnings are not cut back, so they won't fit smoothly in the crotch area.

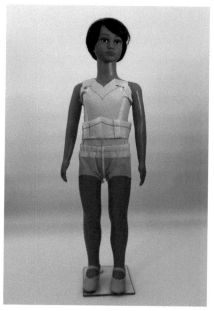

Check the leg line on the body. Remember not to make the area at the front of the leg too high or it will be too shallow to accommodate all the net layers.

Finally, pin the waist of the bodice to the lower edge of the waist Petersham, starting at the CF, temporarily pinning the CBs (it is easier to fit if these pins are removed once the correct alignment of bodice and basque is established), and then distribute the rest of the bodice on the basque, matching the SSs. As the bodice sits over the basque, it should be very slightly eased onto the basque.

If sleeves are part of the costume, fit them at the second fitting when the bodice and tutu plate will already be established and their effect and proportion can be looked at as a whole.

The first fitting

Make sure you are well prepared for the fitting. You will need a tape measure, scissors, pins, safety pins, pencil, notebook, design sketch or reference, and of course the toile. A camera is also useful to take photographs of any areas that need attention. This is especially important if you are making a set of tutus.

Ideally the fitting will take place in a room with a full-length mirror. Check the dancer's name when they arrive – I once assumed they were coming in fitting order, but two dancers I hadn't met before swapped places and consequently got fitted in each other's toile.

Pin down the CB of the basque. Ideally this will be along the machine-marked line, but if the waistband has been adjusted, the basque CB will need to be adjusted by a similar amount. Now check the fit of the rest of the basque so it lies smoothly; you may need to adjust the side seam or take a pleat out of the high hip edge to achieve this. Use safety pins to make the right shape for the dancer's body. The bodice will require peeling up so you can see if the basque sits properly.

Now pass the crotch tape through the legs and pin it to the junction where the high hip line meets the CB. Ask the dancer if they feel comfortable – check the waistband is still comfortable and doesn't need adjusting. Also check the high hip line is level and running parallel to the floor – if the dancer is sway-waisted or has a pronounced or small bottom, or wide or narrow hips, you may need to adjust the high hip line to ensure the tutu does not tip. Mark the new line with a pencil if necessary.

If you made the decision to fit the knicker without the net attached, check it at this stage. It should not be tight, but fit comfortably. Check the leg line – how does it fit over the bottom? Although in the finished tutu most of this knicker will not be seen, in its naked state a dancer may ask for a higher leg at the front. Be wary about making this much higher as there needs to be enough space to add all the net layers. (There is further discussion on this in the 'Trouble-shooting' section at the end of Chapter 5.)

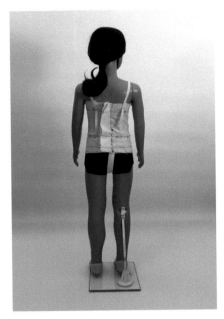

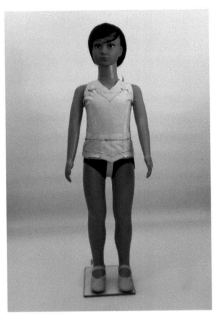

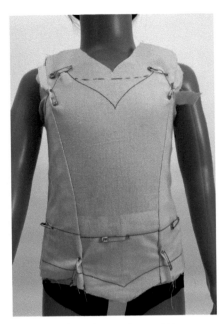

Pin along the CB, making adjustments if necessary. Check the shoulder elastic length so the bodice sits smoothly on the body.

Check the fit at the front – does it need adjustment on any of the seams?

Mark any alteration to the neckline straight onto the calico using pencil.

Now fit the bodice. Begin by pinning the waist together at the CB. Check the shoulder elastics and adjust if necessary. Now pin the rest of the CB together: ideally it should do up on the marked lines, but don't force it. It is helpful to have a full-length mirror for the dancer to observe how they look and it is useful to get a little distance as this can highlight any problems. Look at the overall effect. Then look at the fit of the front. Start by checking that the bust is in the correct position for the bodice and adjust by taking a pleat or marking the nipple point with a pencil mark if it is higher. Does the bodice fit neatly over the bust? Ideally, you should try to avoid altering the CF panel unless the point-to-point (the position of the dancer's bust) needs adjusting. If there is too much fabric in the bust area, take a pleat out of the SF panel. Ask the dancer if they feel comfortable – check the shoulder elastics and basque waistband are still correct and adjust if required. When you are happy that the shell of the bodice fits snuggly to the body, you can start to look at the design lines.

Have a look at the neckline – is it flattering and at the right height? Get the dancer to do a back bend and use the épaulement to make sure her nipples don't appear over the proposed thread-marked finish line – pencil any alterations straight onto the calico. If a 'V'-shaped CF neckline is desired, it may be necessary to add an infill to keep the bodice in shape; pencil the neckline onto the calico in preparation for making a pattern from the negative shape. This will be checked at the second fitting. Look at where the top line finishes on the back: it

shouldn't hamper the shoulder blade but sit either above or below it, so adjust if necessary.

I have made costumes for several dancers with conditions like scoliosis or marked asymmetry, for instance due to different shoulder heights. Sometimes the dancer will be open about this. If they are not forthcoming, do not draw attention to it, but consider if it will be necessary to make uneven adjustments to the costume.

A final check

Stand back and check the overall effect by looking at the dancer in the mirror. It may be that the designer has already determined the depth of the tutu, but if you have a private commission, have a look at the proportions on the dancer and decide now how far you would like it to stick out from the high hip line. If making a tutu for a competition, check it complies with the governing body's requirements.

When I am happy I have a good fit, I like to take photographs of the front, back and side views of the dancer in the toile which can be referred to later if there is something I need to check. Always ask if the dancer is happy to be photographed, and consider taking pictures of just the costume excluding their face if they would prefer this. If you are fitting more than one dancer, be sure to also take a photo of their name pencilled on the CB so you can identify them later. To protect the privacy of dancers, I always discard fitting photographs once the costume is complete and I no longer require them.

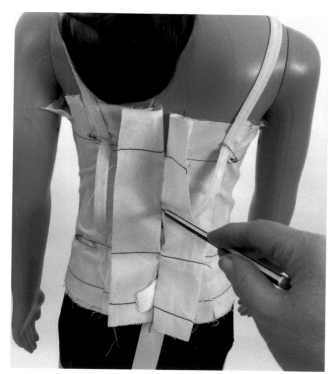

When you are happy with the fit, mark the CB of both sides of the bodice before removing the safety pins.

It is impossible to make a wrinkle-free bodice for a dancer! The finished costume should be able to move with the dancer and be comfortable. Yes, it should look as smooth as possible when the dancer is standing still, but any movement or bending associated with dance will result in some wrinkling. This is not an excuse for a badly fitting bodice, but it is important to manage dancers' expectations.

Use pencil to mark the position of the pins on both sides of the CB bodice. Don't worry if it looks a bit wrinkled at this stage; it will be boned when finished which will smooth it out. Then mark the CB of the basque. Leave all other pins in the bodice until you are ready to deal with the alterations.

I always write notes about the fitting immediately. It is very easy to forget a specific request from a dancer, and if you are fitting more than one costume it is even more important to make notes, especially if there are a few days between the fitting and starting the next stage of construction. Use a page per dancer, add the date, any comments from the dancer and any distinguishing notes (for example, was wearing pink legwarmers, mentioned liking strawberries ...) which can be useful to nudge your memory later.

Altering the patterns

Marking up the corrected patterns

Before starting to correct the toile after fitting, assemble the notes and any photos from the fitting. Look at the toile, and then unpin the basque from the bodice.

The altered calico toile can be used as the pattern; it cuts out a process and the inaccuracies associated with transferring it to paper. The tracing wheel can be quite brutal to paper and calico is quite stable as long as you leave the seam allowances attached. But do transfer the finished pattern to paper if you prefer.

Measure the fitted length of the waistband and make a note of it, then unpick the Petersham tape from the basque. Are alterations to the basque needed? Even up any fitting differences between the right and left of the calico basque sections and adjust evenly; add up the measurement of both sides and divide by two. It is important that the CB remains on the straight grain, at 90 degrees to the waistline, so if during the fitting it has moved out of line, adjust the side seams to account for the difference. Did you need to take small darts on the high hip to make it fit? Unless the dancer is particularly curvaceous, it shouldn't be necessary to put actual darts into the finished pattern, so if you come across this situation, stitch them into the calico and press flat before redrafting the high hip line to smooth it out. Did the high hip line sit horizontally or did you need to re-mark it lower at the side seams or around the back? Redraft this if necessary following the pencil lines from the fitting.

Then turn your attention to the bodice. As with the basque, mark and then even up any safety-pinned alterations with a pencil. Separate the panels and press them flat with an iron – you need work on only one half of the bodice. Keep the CB on the straight-of-grain, which may necessitate making the adjustment on the CB/SB seam or the side seam.

Keep the waistline where it is, and begin by altering the vertical seams according to any alteration marks. The waist side seam should sit half way between the CF and CB: take the waist measurement of the bodice from the fitting and the length of the CF to SS and SS to CB should be a quarter of this measurement, so it marries nicely with the basque underneath.

The bodice will need to be slightly bigger than the basque it goes over, so check the waist and high hip measurements are about 1.5cm bigger to allow for this.

When you are happy with the vertical alterations, pin the bodice together smoothly and re-mark the top line if necessary. Add in balance marks before unpinning the corrected pattern in readiness for cutting out.

Correcting the knicker pattern

Select the knicker pattern that corresponds most closely to the measurements of your dancer. The patterns can be found on pages 29 and 30 and are based on a grid of 2.5cm; you will notice the pattern is half a knicker as it will be seamed down the CF. Note also that the pattern is divided into eighths: it is within these vertical lines that each of your sections of pleated net will be added.

Measure the length of the high hip line on your altered basque and then add 2cm ease. This ease is important as although the bobbinet fabric has a little stretch, the finished knicker should not be tight when you stitch it to the basque. Divide this measurement by 2; this is the length the high hip line of the knicker pattern should measure.

If you need to adjust this knicker pattern circumference, rule a horizontal line across the centre of the pattern as any adjustments should sit along this plane.

As an example, let's say the high hip measurement of the dancer is 6cm larger than the pattern and we also need to add 2cm ease – a total of 8cm. So we need to add 1cm per eighth of the pattern to make a larger circumference. The pattern is already divided eighths so begin slashing down the centre of these eighths. The advantage of correcting the pattern between the eighths is that the width of the crotch remains the same. Rule a horizontal line across a new piece of pattern paper in order to keep all the pattern pieces in the correct plane. Spread each of the slashes 1cm to make a total of 4cm visible on the half pattern knowing this will total the 8cm we need in the finished knicker. Use sticky tape to stick the pieces down and redraft the missing lines.

Use a similar method if the pattern needs to be made smaller, but this time lapping the pattern pieces over each other in equal proportions to reduce the size.

Now check the hip is the correct size. Take the waist to hip depth measurement from your chart. Remembering to make allowance for the depth of the basque (5cm/6.25cm/7.5cm), subtract this, and then measure the knicker pattern down vertically from the high hip line and make a dot with a pencil. Now take the fullest hip measurement from your measurement sheet, add 2cm ease and then divide in half and measure horizontally across the pattern to check the pattern is large enough to accommodate the hips. If you need to make increase the size, slightly splay the back section of the pattern before re-marking the high hip with a straight line. Do the reverse if it needs to be smaller.

Now check the girth is correct. Measure the crotch elastic or Petersham ribbon from the fitting and add 1.5cm for ease and compare this to the CF and CB

Tip

Marking out the net layer lines on the paper pattern with the tracing wheel can damage it. Even though you can tape it back together, you may want to make a master pattern from net, which will be much more robust if you envisage using it more than once, and has the added advantage of transparency, which can be useful for checking the accuracy of the knicker during its construction.

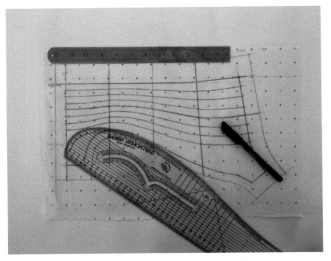

Copying the finished pattern onto nylon net will ensure its longevity, especially if it will be used more than once.

pattern length. The simplest way to adjust this is to raise or lower the high hip line accordingly. Mark this new line with a pen and ruler.

The layer lines will need adjusting if you have altered your pattern. Note where the Layer 4 line falls – this is important as the CB opening will start above it. Look at its position and check that the proportions of your pattern echo those of the diagram.

If you have altered the pattern around the circumference of the body, you will need to join up the layer lines on a new pattern; I like to lightly draw them in by eye, and then refine them using a French curve. Be careful that the Layer 1 line allows sufficient distance from the finished knicker leg to stitch on a bias channel to hold the knicker elastic.

If you have altered the girth, keep Layers 4 to 1 in the same place, and spread or narrow the lines above by evenly dividing the spaces on the eighth lines and then linking them as before – initially by eye, and then refining them with a French curve.

The most important lines and the ones you will later machine thread-mark are shown in bold.

If you made the decision to fit the knicker at the first fitting, use the information gained to transfer any alterations onto the pattern.

Note the horizontal line in red across the centre of the pattern, which is used to keep the alterations in the same plane. The vertical lines divide the pattern into eighths, so that adjustments can be made equally across the pattern.

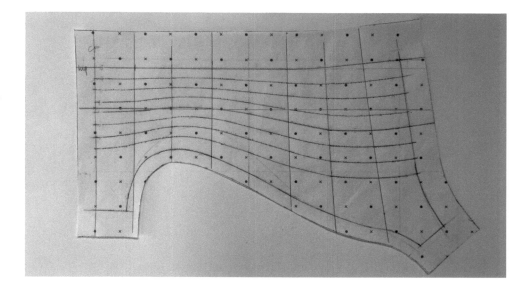

The pattern has been made smaller by overlapping each of the sections and taping together.

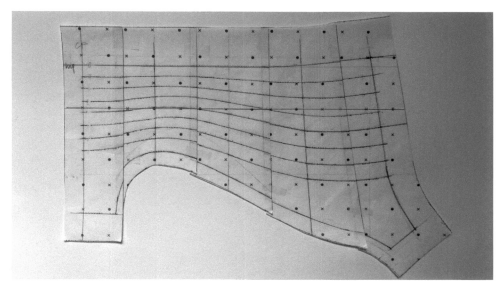

This pattern has been made larger by spreading the pattern pieces before taping onto a larger sheet of paper.

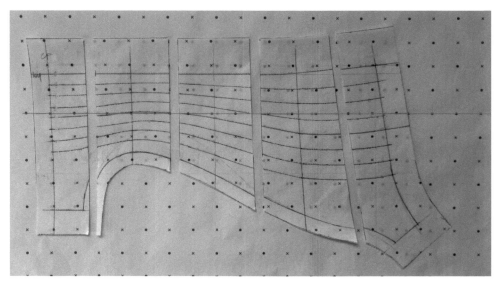

The net recipe

A tutu recipe is a table which contains a series of measurements and instructions for each graduated layer of net. The deepest and longest layer will be attached at the high hip line, with the depth and quantity of the net diminishing as the net layers descend the knicker until they reach the knicker leg.

Three different recipes are illustrated here.

It is useful to format a similar document on your computer. This not only enables you to keep a record of your work, but also makes it easy to adapt for future use. The table shows a basic document which can be copied and printed off, and the labels separated and pinned to each net layer as it is cut. It is vital each cut layer of net is labelled as they look similar and can easily become muddled.

The recipe is designed for net which is 150cm or 54in wide. This is a standard width, but if you happen to have a different width net, you will need to recalibrate the recipe to work out how many widths are in your new net; the quantity diminishes as the layers go down the body – work to the nearest quarter of a width if the answer is a fraction.

The instructions within each rectangle on the table refer to:

Layer – the position on the knicker where the pleated nets are applied: the higher the number, the nearer the net is to the high hip line, and the lower the number, the closer it is to the crotch seam.

Depth – the depth of the skirt, or the distance it extends from the body.

Length – the finished length of each layer, which will be pleated to fit onto the knicker.

Width – the number of 150cm widths in each layer. You will notice that in the child's recipe, for example, layer 8 is not only the longest net, but also contains the most fabric: three widths of 1.5m wide net, so there is a total of 4.5m in the top layer. The quantity of net contained in each layer diminishes as it travels down the knicker. This quantity will need adjusting in the event the fabric used is a different width.

Point/scallop – apply a pointed or scalloped finish to the outside edge of the net to give your tutus a professional look. I use a selection of three different-sized templates depending on the tutu size made, marked on the recipe as large (L), medium (M), small (S) or extra small (XS). Use the largest size template for the upper nets.

Down or up – the direction in which the net is stitched onto the knicker. Sewing the lower layers on so they point up gives additional 'lift' to the plate.

Stiff or soft – a stiff net helps the tutu to maintain its shape, but can be very uncomfortable and scratchy around the dancer's legs. For this reason, the leg ruffles and some of the lower layers are made from a softer net.

Channel – the channel is a strip of net that is stitched onto the centre of one of the middle net layers to provide a conduit to contain a hoop. This helps with the stability and longevity of the tutu. Even if you think you do not want to insert a hoop, I recommend adding the channel at this stage as it is virtually impossible to add one later. In the event your tutu becomes a bit floppy over time, it will be an easy enough process to revive it by inserting a hoop, resteaming and restringing.

Colour – if you are making a coloured tutu, you may wish to grade the net colours. You can afford to have quite strong contrasts as the net in a single layer will look quite pale. Subtlety quickly vanishes under stage lights.

It is also useful to add the dancer's name to each label if you are making a set of several different-sized tutus.

Recipe for an adult 12-layer tutu

Height 165cm; 38cm deep

High Hip Layer: 12
Depth: 38cm
Widths: 5
Scallop: L
Down
Stiff

Layer: 11
Depth: 35cm
Widths: 4.5
Scallop: L
Down
Stiff

Layer: 10
Depth: 32cm
Widths: 4
Scallop: L
Down
Stiff

Layer: 9
Depth: 29cm
Widths: 3.75
Scallop: L
Down
Stiff

Layer: 8
Depth: 26cm
Widths: 3.5
Scallop: L
Down
Stiff

Layer: 7
Depth 23cm
Widths: 3.25
Scallop: L
Down
Stiff
Channel

Layer: 6
Depth: 20cm
Widths: 3
Scallop: M
Down
Stiff

Layer: 5
Depth: 17cm
Widths: 2.75
Scallop: M
Down
Soft

Layer: 4
Depth: 14cm
Widths: 2.5
Scallop: M
Up
Stiff

Layer: 3
Depth: 11cm
Widths: 2.25
Scallop: M
Up
Soft

Layer: 2
Depth: 8cm
Widths: 2
Scallop: S
Up
Stiff

Layer: 1
Depth: 4.5cm
Widths: 2
Scallop: S
Up
Soft

Layer: Leg Ruffle
Length: 2.5cm
Widths: 2.5
Scallop: S
Up
Soft

Layer: Channel
Depth: 2.5cm
Widths: 3.25
Stiff

Recipe for a teenage 10-layer tutu

Height 155cm; 34cm deep

High Hip Layer: 10 Depth: 34cm Widths: 4 Scallop: L Down Stiff	Layer: 9 Depth: 30.5cm Widths: 3.75 Scallop: L Down Stiff	Layer: 8 Depth: 27cm Widths: 3.5 Scallop: L Down Stiff	Layer: 7 Depth: 23.5cm Widths: 3.25 Scallop: L Down Stiff Channel
Layer: 6 Depth: 20cm Widths: 3 Scallop: M Down Stiff	Layer: 5 Depth: 16.5cm Widths: 2.75 Scallop: M Down Stiff	Layer: 4 Depth: 13cm Widths: 2.5 Scallop: M Up Stiff	Layer: 3 Depth: 10cm Widths: 2.25 Scallop: M Up Soft
Layer: 2 Depth: 7cm Widths: 2 Scallop: S Up Stiff	Layer: 1 Depth: 4cm Widths: 2 Scallop: S Up Soft	Layer: Leg Ruffle Length: 2.5cm Widths: 2.5 Scallop: S Up Soft	Layer 7: Channel Depth: 2.5cm Widths: 3.25 Stiff

Height 130cm; 27cm deep

High Hip Layer: 8 Depth: 27cm Widths: 3 Scallop: M Down Stiff	Layer: 7 Depth: 24cm Widths: 2.75 Scallop: M Down Stiff	Layer: 6 Depth: 21cm Widths: 2.5 Scallop: M Down Stiff Channel	Layer: 5 Depth: 18cm Widths: 2.25 Scallop: M Down Stiff
Layer: 4 Depth: 14cm Widths: 2 Scallop: S Down Stiff	Layer: 3 Depth: 10cm Widths: 1.75 Scallop: S Up Soft	Layer: 2 Depth: 7cm Widths: 1.5 Scallop: S Up Stiff	Layer: 1 Depth: 4cm Widths: 1.5 Scallop: XS Up Soft
Layer: Leg Ruffle Length: 2.5cm Widths: 2.5 Scallop: XS Up Soft	Layer 6: Channel Depth: 2.5cm Widths: 2.5 Stiff		

Altering the net recipe

Having completed the first fitting, you will have an idea of what shape and how deep you would like the tutu plate to be. The recipe will be the same whether you are making a plate/pancake or drop/bell shape. This shaping is created later in the process when the tutu is strung together.

The recipes given here should suit most purposes, but you will need to consider the height and age of the dancer before assessing whether you need to refine them. If you are making for a professional company, the designer and choreographer will want to have some input. The depths and style of a tutu change with fashion, so these recipes are just a suggestion. Feel free to adjust them to your own needs.

If making a set of tutus, create a chart containing all the dancers' measurements. It is only the top four or so layers that need adjustment; lower layers can remain the same. The given widths and lengths can also remain the same.

Let's take as an example creating a 12-layer tutu for a 155cm tall dancer with the recipe designed for a dancer 165cm in height. Understand that removing 2cm from the depth of the high hip layer will visually reduce the tutu's width by 4cm, so small increments make a difference, but this ratio should work for a dancer who is 10cm shorter than the recipe has been created for. If Layer 12 is reduced by 2cm, to leave a depth of 36cm, the following layers need adjustment until they merge into the lower layers of the tutu. Looking at the original recipe, you can see that each layer reduces in depth by 3cm. If instead the reduction is 2.5cm, that would leave Layer 12 at 36cm, Layer 11 at 33.5cm, Layer 10 at 31cm and Layer 9 at 28.5cm. A further reduction of 2.5cm for Layer 8 will total 26cm, which is in line with the original recipe.

Conversely, increasing the depth of this 12-layer tutu recipe by 2cm could be done as follows: Layer 12 at 40cm, Layer 11 at 36.5cm, Layer 10 at 33cm and Layer 9 at 29.5cm, returning again to the regular recipe with Layer 8 at 26cm. In this case, the increases are 3.5cm. It doesn't always work out so neatly, but use your judgement: 5mm here or there won't make much difference in the finished costume.

Be wary of making the tutu any deeper than 40cm as the longer it is, the more engineering support it will need to stay up, and at this depth it is nearing its maximum viability.

For younger dancers, some dance competitions have specific rules for tutu length, and it is worth checking this first – some like the length of the tutu to reach the fingertips when the arms are outstretched; some prefer it shorter.

Colour grading

You can of course use contrasting colours, or subtle changes in colour. Be aware that in a single layer, other than at the dense pleated head, the net quickly loses the intensity of the colour seen in the bolt.

Grading the colours of the net layers can be very effective. Let's take as an example grading the plate from orange, through apricot to pale apricot at the knicker on a 12-layer tutu.

Due to the combination of stiff and soft net, it will simplify things if all the soft net is cut in one colour. So in this case the leg ruffle and Layers 1, 3 and 5 are cut in the pale apricot. The remaining layers need blending together through to the high hip. This could mean using the mid-tone for Layers 2, 4, 6, 8 and 10 and the darkest orange tone for Layers 7 (including the channel), 9, 11 and 12.

Dye the knicker a similar colour as the first few layers (1–3), as this is where it will be most visible, and then the first couple of layers should merge into the costume. There may of course be a design decision to have dramatic contrasts between the net and the knicker colour.

Altered depth recipe for an adult 12-layer tutu

Height 155cm; 36cm deep

High Hip Layer	Depth	Width	Scallop	Direction	Stiff or Soft
12	36cm	5	Large	Down	Stiff
11	33.5cm	4.5	Large	Down	Stiff
10	31cm	4	Large	Down	Stiff
9	28.5cm	3.75	Large	Down	Stiff
8	26cm	3.5	Large	Down	Stiff
7	23cm	3.25	Large	Down	Stiff
					Channel
6	20cm	3	Medium	Down	Stiff
5	17cm	2.75	Medium	Down	Soft
4	14cm	2.5	Medium	Up	Stiff
3	11cm	2.25	Medium	Up	Soft
2	8cm	2	Small	Up	Stiff
1	4.5cm	2	Small	Up	Soft
Leg ruffle	2.5cm	2.5	Small	Up	Soft
Layer 7 Channel	2.5cm	3.25			Stiff

Recipe for a colour-graded adult 12-layer tutu

Height 165cm; 38cm deep

High Hip Layer	Depth	Width	Scallop	Direction	Stiff or Soft	Colour
12	38cm	5	Large	Down	Stiff	Orange
11	35cm	4.5	Large	Down	Stiff	Orange
10	32cm	4	Large	Down	Stiff	Apricot
9	29cm	3.75	Large	Down	Stiff	Orange
8	26cm	3.5	Large	Down	Stiff	Apricot
7	23cm	3.25	Large	Down	Stiff	Orange
					Channel	
6	20cm	3	Medium	Down	Stiff	Apricot
5	17cm	2.75	Medium	Down	Soft	Pale apricot
4	14cm	2.5	Medium	Up	Stiff	Apricot
3	11cm	2.25	Medium	Up	Soft	Pale apricot
2	8cm	2	Small	Up	Stiff	Apricot
1	4.5cm	2	Small	Up	Soft	Pale apricot
Leg ruffle	2.5cm	2.5	Small	Up	Soft	Pale apricot
Layer 7 Channel	2.5cm	3.25			Stiff	Orange

CHAPTER 3

The Tutu Plate

You will have made several important design decisions which affect the final look of your tutu by this stage. Having completed the first fitting and subsequent pattern alterations, you will now be ready to launch into constructing the tutu plate.

Cutting out the nets

The instructions below are based on the recipe for a child's 8-layer tutu.

STEP 1: Print off a copy of your final tutu recipe document and separate the labels. Start by sorting them into net types – stiff or soft net – and if you are varying the colours, also separate these into piles. It is useful to have a long table on which to cut the nets out as this makes the process more efficient.

Put aside the soft net labels for Layers 3, 1 and the leg ruffles. Take the remaining stiff net labels, high hip Layer 8 (27cm), Layer 7 (24cm), Layer 6 (21cm), channel for Layer 6 (2.5cm), Layer 5 (18cm), Layer 4 (14cm) and Layer 2 (7cm). Add together the depths of the stiff net, which in this case totals 113.5cm. If the cutting-out table is longer than this, all the layers can be cut out at the same time. If it is shorter, begin by grouping together the higher, deeper layers and stop when the total exceeds the table length.

STEP 2: Begin by cutting the deepest layers first, as any leftovers from cutting half or quarter sections can be recycled for use in the lower layers. Unroll several metres of the stiff net from the bolt. If the net comes unfolded on a roll, it is much more manageable if you fold it in half before marking out.

Lay the net flat on the table. Align the folded edge with the table's edge and weight down the net in various places to keep it flat.

As an example, what follows are the instructions to economically cut out the 8-layer child's tutu. It will initially seem complicated, but read the instructions first and give it a go. You can always work out your own method of cutting which makes sense to you. As long as you end up with the correct length and depth in each layer, it will work.

STEP 3: Start by ruling a square end with your 'L' square with a vanishing fabric marker. Measure from this first line and mark across the net with the 'L' square at 113.5cm, plus 1.5cm margin for error, a total of 115cm: depth required for the stiff net layers. Cut across at this line. Place another layer of net on top of this first length, cutting both off neatly at 115cm, using the weights to keep everything flat and together so there are two equal, accurate layers. Next add together the depth of those layers that need just 2.25 or fewer widths: Layer 2 (depth: 7cm) 1.5 widths, Layer 4 (depth: 14cm) 2 widths, Layer 5 (depth: 18cm) 2.25 widths. The

total depth required for these layers is 39cm. Draw a line across at this level, but do not cut it. The remaining layers have a maximum of 3 widths, so place a further layer of net on top of the first two layers, starting from this 39cm line and extending the remaining 76cm length of the fabric on the table. This will result in 115cm net on the table, 39cm of which has two layers, and the remaining 76cm with 3 layers. Move the weights as you go, and if necessary add the odd pin.

STEP 4: Layer 8 is the only layer requiring exactly 3 widths of net, so draw a line 27cm from the end that has three layers of net. Pin the Layer 8 label to the top edge and then add pins to the lower edge of the layer; at this stage it is good to be aware of the next process – cutting out the decorative edge. With this in mind, place the pins on this lower edge sufficiently far away from its edge that they will not need to be moved when cutting out the scallops or points. Then pin beyond the line at the bottom of Layer 8 with just enough pins to keep Layer 7 together, and cut along the line to release the uppermost layer of the tutu.

STEP 5: Now tackle Layer 7 (depth: 24cm, 2.75 layers). Draw a line 24cm from the previously cut edge, but before pinning across, a quarter of a width needs to be removed. Do this by adjusting the weights and folding the whole uppermost length of the net layer towards you. As it is already folded in half, cut down this fold down until you hit the 24cm line. Unfold and attach the Layer 7 label, again pinning the lower edge ensuring not to include the quarter width which will come away as you cut along the 24cm line. Continue with this method to cut Layer 6 and the Layer 6 channel, which require 2.5 widths, slicing down the folded edge. Layer 5 will require an extra quarter of a width which can be harvested from the fabric removed from Layer 7. Layer 4 is simple with just two widths, and half a width will need to be removed for Layer 2.

By the end of this process, all the stiff layers of net should be neatly piled up in order, labelled, and with one edge containing a row of pins set back from the edge in preparation for pointing or scalloping.

Now repeat the process with the soft net, which will be mathematically much simpler, but the narrower the depth, the fiddlier the layers become. You will find it easier to leave layer 1 and the leg ruffles attached in pairs, scallop each edge and then separate them afterwards. If you are making a set of tutus, cut all the Layer 8s at the same time, followed by all the Layer 7s, and so

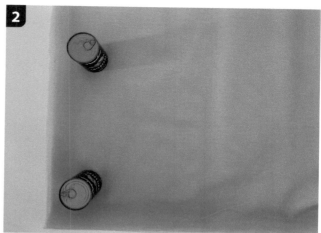

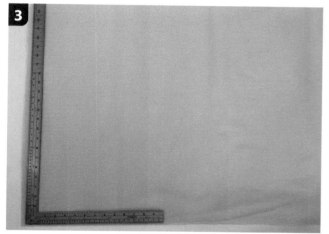

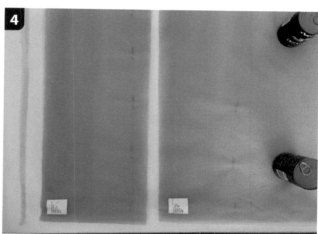

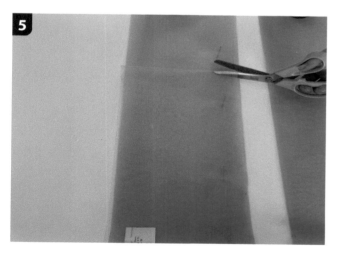

on. This is a more efficient way of working and enables the deeper discarded half and quarter offcuts to be economically used for the narrower lower layers.

Some tutu-makers like to cut each layer lengthwise down the net. If you wish to do this, sample the pleating process before making this decision as sometimes the net doesn't pleat as well along the warp. You will still need to pin them together to cut the points, and there will be a little more wastage if you do it this way.

Cutting the decorative edge – scallops or points?

STEP 1: Decide on the decorative edge you prefer and prepare your own templates from card, or photocopy the images opposite and paste onto card. As a guide, make the large edge about 4cm wide and deep, the medium edge 2.5cm and the small edge 1.5cm. (There are photocopiable templates for scallops and points at the back of the book.)

STEP 2: Separate the net layers into piles for the point sizes needed according to the recipe used: large (L), medium (M), small (S) and extra small (XS).

STEP 3: Start with the deepest layer and place the largest template required by your recipe onto the pinned edge of the net, with the template just over the edge of the net. Using a pencil or vanishing pen, trace around the template points or scallops so the marks will be removed as the edge is cut out, leaving behind an accurate edge without losing any of the depth.

STEP 4: Cut the layers as efficiently as possible using paper scissors, as cutting this density of net is likely to blunt your best fabric scissors. To cut points, clip one side of the point down the length of the net, then go back and cut the other side, thereby releasing the resultant remnant triangle. With scallops, it is also easier to clip the curve on one side all the way down the length and then go back and cut the other side. You will find that pointed edges easily pick up small pieces of thread or net, so brush these onto the floor to sweep up later. Do be careful, though, as they can make a hard floor very slippery.

The deepest layer contains the most net, so it is the most difficult to cut. The layers become easier to cut as they contain fewer widths. As you get down to the smaller layers, it is possible to fold them again and therefore have half the distance to cut. Separate the soft, small layers you have left in pairs and pile up the layers in order. Leave the channel without an edge.

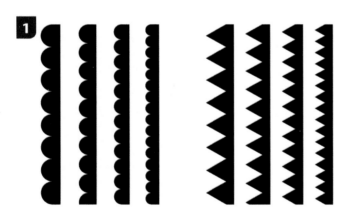

Tip

Don't wear your best knitwear or delicate fabrics while you are making a tutu base as the net snags on them. Long sleeves will protect your arms from scratches or irritation if you have delicate skin.

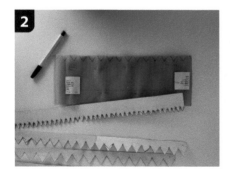
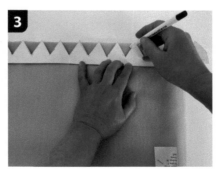

Making the knicker

Preparing the bobbinet

The bobbinet fabric is too fine to use in a single layer, so it needs to be cut double. The fabric will shrink, so it is important to wash it before cutting it out. It will not look as pristine after laundering, and in my experience it can distort slightly and stretch at the edges, so arrange the bobbinet in a double layer, matching the grainlines, before immersing it in water. It is not necessary to wash it in a washing machine – a hand-wash using hot water should be sufficient – and then spin in a spinner or use the rinse and spin function of a washing machine, ensuring it is laid flat in the machine in an attempt to avoid it ending up in a creased tangle. Iron two layers of bobbinet together, aiming to match the selvedges and horizontal grainlines.

Cutting out the bobbinet

The bobbinet has a one-way stretch, which will sit horizontally around the body. It will help when you come to stitch on the high hip layer net if you have left a little spare at the top, so leave any excess in the knowledge that this section will be cut away later. You may find a more economical layout is to tessellate the pieces. Luckily the textile is quite 'sticky' and well-behaved, so you shouldn't need many pins. Cut out two double layers with about 2cm allowance everywhere except the high hip line, where you could leave up to 8cm extra.

Marking up the bobbinet

STEP 1: Lay the two double sections of bobbinet exactly on top of one another (a total of four layers of fabric). Check that they sit happily on top of one another and nothing is stretched or rucked. You now need to transfer the pattern markings to what will become the outside of your knicker. It is important to ensure that all the lines

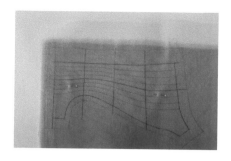

Pinning the pattern to the bobbinet.

are accurately marked at this stage as any inaccuracies will compound as you go through the project and make fitting difficult at the later stages. Pin the pattern onto the fabric – I like to do this about halfway across the pattern. This means you can then 'peel back' one double layer and insert the folded carbon paper to mark both layers at once. Lay the fabric and pattern back over the paper, ensuring everything is flat, accurate and neat, and that the cut bobbinet aligns once again. Mark using a tracing wheel with a smooth profile – if you use one that has sharp points, they tend to find the holes in the fabric and not transfer the markings consistently.

STEP 2: All of the pattern lines need transferring: the CF and CB, the knicker leg, the crotch seams, each of the horizontal lines upon which the net layers sit, and finally the vertical 'eighth' lines which are used to check each section contains a similar amount of pleated net. For white knickers, use yellow carbon paper as it is almost invisible in the finished garment.

STEP 3: The majority of these chalk-marked lines now need marking with a machine stitch. This stitching not only links the double layer of fabric together, it also aids visibility of the lines and adds strength. The example shows contrasting stitching for clarity, but you should use matching-coloured polyester thread which will not hamper the stretch of the knicker or be visible in the final garment.

It is important to test the stitching does not distort the fabric and make the knicker smaller than the pattern, so begin by testing a medium-sized straight stitch on two layers of scrap fabric. It is unnecessary to use any

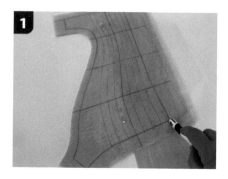

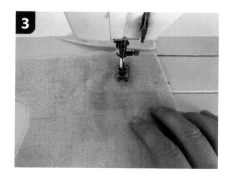

backstitching, but stitch from raw edge to raw edge, keeping an eye on the tension as you go. For efficient sewing, stitch one line after the other like bunting and snip as you go. This adds speed, saves thread, and stops the creation of small thread ends which will later get swept up and collected by the tutu net.

Not all the marked layer lines need stitching, just those marked in bold on the pattern: the horizontal lines which need stitching are the high hip line, depending on the size either Layer 3 or 4 – whichever indicates the base of the CB opening, as this also marks where the first net layer is attached – the front and back crotch lines and knicker leg lines. The vertical lines which need stitching are the CF, CB and the 'eighth' lines. Each stitch line should be a separate line of sewing to avoid constricting the fabric, and allow you to pull the fabric piece back into shape if the stitch line distorts it. Lay the two finished knicker sections flat on the ironing board and compare them to the pattern. As the knicker leg is on the bias, it is vulnerable to distortion, so as a guide use the straight high hip line, which follows the weft grainline, then the CF and CB lines to compare with the pattern. With these pressed in place, shrink any stretched sections back using steam from the iron, ensuring you end up with both pieces the same shape.

STEP 4: The knicker is now ready to be assembled and a French seam is a neat way to finish the CF. Begin by placing the two knicker sections on top of one another, unmarked sides together. Pin exactly on the finished CF line, matching the horizontal high hip and crotch thread marks accurately. The fabric does not stretch in the warp, so adjust the machine to a medium-sized straight stitch and test this on two layers of fabric using polyester thread, ensuring the stitch line does not tighten up.

STEP 5: Begin the seam with the first line of stitching about 5mm outside the CF, into the seam allowance. The presser foot on my machine lines up nicely so I am able to line up the outer edge of the foot to the CF line, but your machine may differ. Stitch from raw edge to raw edge, backstitching only within the borders of the finished knicker; most of the seam allowances will be trimmed away, so it's important this backstitch locks the areas which are likely to be under most strain in the finished garment.

STEP 6: Trim the seam allowance back neatly to 3mm.

STEP 7: Press the machined stitching line flat first. Next open up the seam and press firstly to one side, and then fold under the seam allowance in half so the unmarked or wrong side (WS) is showing and the knicker pieces sit flat on top of each other.

STEP 8: The second line of stitching goes on top of the thread-marked CF, so pin and then stitch on this line, again backstitching within the pattern pieces, effectively trapping the raw edges of the seam allowances.

STEP 9: Press this seam flat to one side. There are excellent videos online explaining how to construct French seams and they are well worth watching if this technique is new to you.

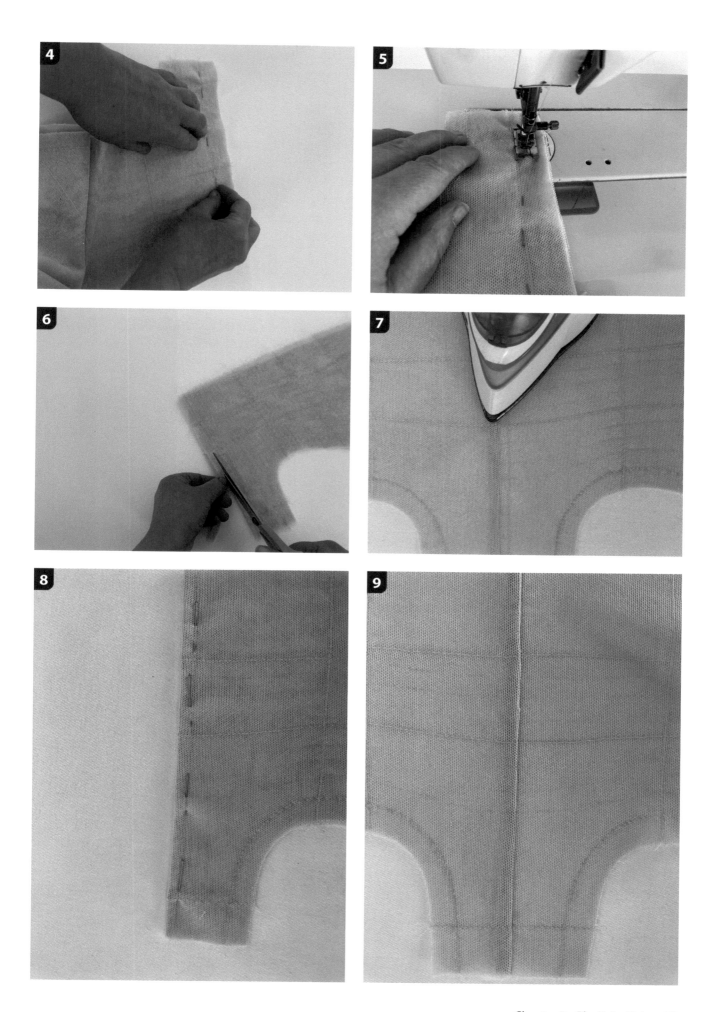

Making the CB opening

STEP 1: The CB knicker opening extends above Layer 3 of the smaller size, and above Layer 4 on the larger sizes. These openings will eventually sit below the basque and meet edge-to-edge with no extension. Neaten the base of this opening by stitching the equivalent of three sides of a buttonhole using a zigzag stitch. This should sit either side of the stitch line which marks the junction of the base of the opening, with the bar section of the buttonhole finishing exactly on the CB and the process starting and finishing at the raw edge. Alternatively, this stage can be done with a buttonhole stitch if your machine has this function. Just omit the final bar.

STEP 2: Cut down the space between the zig zags all the way to the CB, and then trim the allowance from the base of the opening to the top of the knicker to 1.5cm. Leave the seam allowance below this line as it will require another French seam after the tutu nets have been added.

STEP 3: To finish the opening, use an iron to fold both sides along the CB line, and then tuck in the raw edges and press.

STEP 4: Hold the CB opening in place using a straight machine stitch. Start at the raw edge, stitching close to the folded CB edge, across at the base of the opening, and then back up to the raw edge, capturing the folded, pressed edge within the fabric of the knicker. No backstitching is necessary here as it will not be under any strain.

STEP 5: To create the channels that will carry the knicker elastic, trim back the knicker leg seam allowances to 7mm.

STEP 6: Press the raw edge to the inside – that is, the side without the markings. Again, be careful not to stretch the knicker leg edges; check them against the pattern and shrink back using the iron if they have become distorted.

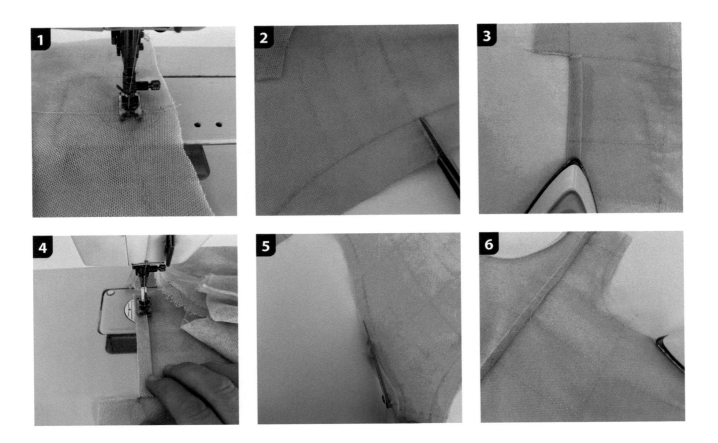

STEP 7: Take the bias binding and neaten the end by folding in 1cm. Use the pattern as a guide and marry one edge of the bias to the edge of the pattern, with the rest of the bias tape occupying the space within the knicker. Begin by setting the folded edge about 5mm back from the crotch line, then mould the binding into the knicker leg shape using the iron. Finish with a fold 5mm before the second crotch line as you need to leave an opening through which to thread the elastic after the crotch seam has been sewn. Repeat for the other leg – remember to make a right and left channel, so either flip the pattern or flip the bias binding before pressing into shape.

STEP 8: Lay the knicker flat on the table and pin the bias binding onto the prepared knicker legs. Set the bias binding 5mm back from the crotch line, pin the tape exactly on the edge of the knicker leg, following the pressed shape you have created. Use a pin at either end, and a couple in the middle. It is likely the knicker will have stretched a little, so if you need to, ease it back under the area which sits under the buttocks. If you take time to prepare the binding carefully with the iron, this process should be swift and result in a neat finish.

STEP 9: By machine-stitching with the bias binding on top, you should be able to adjust any excess bobbinet by gathering it with your fingers and arrange it as it is being stitched; the feed dog on the machine will do the rest of the work for you. Start with the outer edge and edge-stitch as close as you can to the fold of both the bias binding and the knicker. If your sewing machine allows you to alter the needle position, this can be very helpful during this process. It is easier if you start at the raw edge. When you hit the bias binding, backstitch, making a corresponding backstitch when you reach the other end of the binding, and then run off the stitching across the raw edge. Repeat on the other leg before stitching down the remaining inner edges to form a channel. It is wise to check first that the channel created is wide enough to carry your elastic.

STEP 10: The knicker section is now almost complete, so take it back to the ironing board and press it back into shape. Again, check it against the pattern: begin by ensuring the high hip line is still in a straight line, that the CB sections have not splayed and are repositioned if they have, and the knicker leg gets shrunk back to where it should sit.

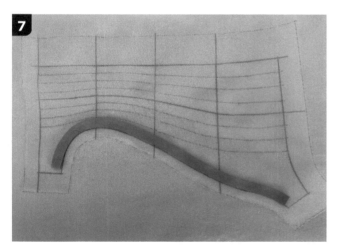

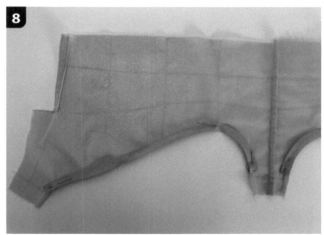

Making the basque and waistband

Basque

The basque section carries the knicker and sits behind the bodice. It is not visible in the finished costume but is important for the stability of the garment as it anchors everything to the waist and ensures it will not shift around in performance.

STEP 1: Using the pre-shrunk drill, fold in half along the warp so that the selvedges meet; the inside will be marked with tracing paper which will sit on the outside of the basque and not be visible in the finished costume, so although it is not vital, it looks neatest if the diagonal weave is visible when you fold the fabric.

Take the basque pattern corrected from the first fitting and pin onto the fabric – the CF needs to go on a fold, and the CB should go on the straight grain – allow an 11cm extension on the CBs, 3cm on the side seams, 1.5cm on the top waist edge and 2.5cm below the high hip line. Mark these seam allowances onto the fabric with a pencil or fabric marker and cut out accurately. As with the knicker, use minimal pinning: two pins in the centre of each piece to ensure it does not twist and enables you to access the lines easily. Then mark using dressmaker's carbon paper sandwiched between the fabric as before; add an extra line 5cm from the CB in the extension allowance. Although one side of the CB will be trimmed back to finish without an extension, it is much less complicated to leave it attached at this stage and remove it later.

STEP 2: Thread-mark with machine stitching. Stitch exactly on top of the following lines: the waistlines, high hip lines, the CF and CBs: only the side seams should be left unmarked. The example shows this done with contrast thread for clarity, but use thread to match the basque colour. The CF line in particular will be useful later when you come to locate the tutu base on the basque.

STEP 3: Neaten the seam allowances by overlocking or zigzagging the sides and top waist – the CB allowance and lower allowance below the high hip line will be dealt with later. Do not cut anything off these seam allowances with the overlocker blade: simply sew over the raw edge of the fabric. It should be possible to neaten the front section in one process; start at the raw edge, overlock up the side, and when the needle has passed the edge of the fabric, stop, raise the presser foot and turn the fabric, siting the blade along the raw edge above the waistline. Continue stitching until the junction with the side is reached, and treat this in a similar way, stitching back to the lower edge. The two back sections require only the side and waist to be overlocked. It is not necessary to knot off the overlocking threads as the cut edges will all be bound or stitched back, but pull them taught and then trim back neatly. Iron the three sections flat.

The finished costume will have a long-line bodice which will come down over this basque section. The side seam (which can be used for future alteration) will sit on the outside – so think of the basque as a lining.

STEP 4: Working out which side of the CB has the extension can be confusing, and it is for this reason I cut the extension on both sides and then cut away the side I don't need at this point.

Roughly pin up both side seams, and with these on the outside, imagine hooking the dancer into the finished basque at the waist: as you look at the basque, the right-hand side is the side that should finish on the CB line and hold the hooks. The left-hand side needs the 5cm extension and will hold the bars. Although you could argue that this is traditionally the men's way to do up a closure, the dancer would find it difficult doing up her own tutu and it is the custom to assume the dresser will be right-handed.

Cut away the excess fabric on the right-hand side leaving a total of 6cm from the CB, remembering that the turnings sit outwards, away from the dancer's body.

STEP 5: Press a fold exactly on the hook side to the marked CB line, and then press under a 1cm turning and pin in place. On the extension side, press back on the stitched line, which is 5cm beyond the CB line, and then turn under a 1cm turning; you can now restitch on the CB line from the RS and trap this edge. It is better to fold these CB fabrics away from the body; the aim is to make the inside as neat and smooth as possible to avoid any discomfort for the dancer.

STEP 6: The two CB sections are now stitched in place. Begin by edge-stitching the folded edges and the turned edges, then stitch a series of adjacent lines each about a machine foot-width apart, about every 5mm to add strength and stability. There is no need to backstitch as these lines will not be under any strain and will be neatened in the next processes. Press these sections flat.

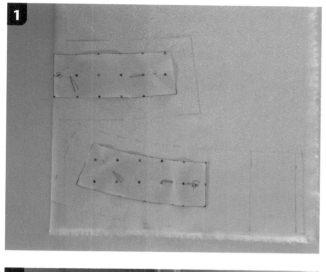

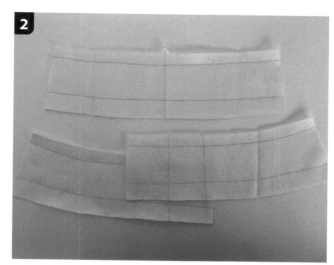

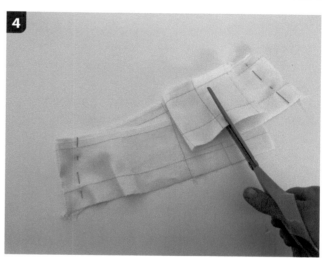

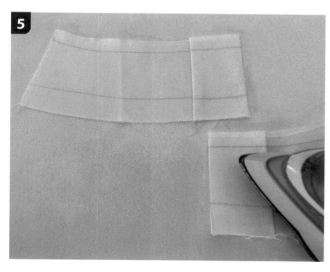

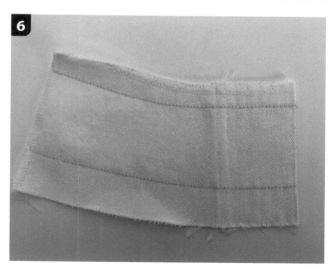

STEP 7: Now neaten the lower edges before the sections are put together. This will make the basque easier to adjust at a later date in the event another dancer needs to wear it, or a young dancer has grown.

Most manufactured bias binding has a small gap between the raw edges. Use this to your advantage when binding the bottom edge of the basque. Estimate the total length of bias you will need for the three sections and press the binding not quite in half, so a lip is evident on one side. Now gently curve this folded bias to echo the shape of the lower edge of the basque, placing the folded edge of the bias along the long edge of the basque. Although this preparation may seem involved, it will aid with the speed, accuracy and finish of the costume.

STEP 8: Take the basque sections and the bias to the sewing machine. Fold in a 1cm bias raw edge to neaten and then slot the binding over the raw edges of each basque section, with the narrowest side uppermost, happy in the knowledge that when you edge-stitch the binding, you will trap the longer lower edge. You may prefer to use a zigzag stitch for this process to make absolutely certain of trapping both sides of the binding. Try not to use pins – you have put all the effort into the preparation so it should stitch on smoothly. Just make sure you don't gather the drill into the binding, making it tight. As you approach the end, cut off the bias with about a 1cm overlap and fold under as before. Repeat with the two other basque sections and then press flat with the iron.

STEP 9: Pin together the side seams. It is important the high hip and waistlines match, and they should sit flat with no ease. Remember these side seams need to be on the outside, so it's a good idea to double-check the right-hand side is still the smaller piece which finishes on the CB before stitching together. Machine-stitch together, backstitching at the bias edge and at the waist. Press the stitching flat and then press the side seam open.

STEP 10: It is a good idea to add hanging tapes at this stage. Cut 2 × 20cm lengths of narrow ribbon or India tape. Fold each in half to create a loop, and pin the two raw edges to meet the overlocked waist edge of the basque on the neatened inside of the side seam, with the folded edges hanging down within the basque in preparation for adding the waistband. In a professional company the tutus will probably be stored on a pole. If it is more likely the tutu will be stored on a hanger, consider stitching these hanging tapes to the lower edge of the basque so the bodice is not distorted during storage.

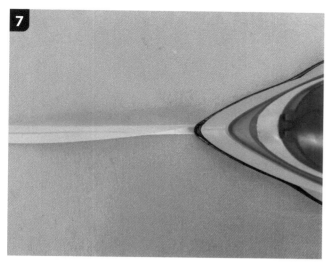

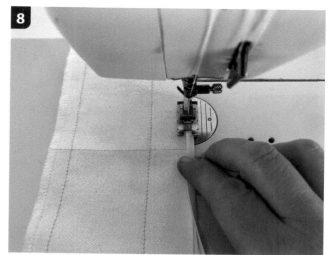

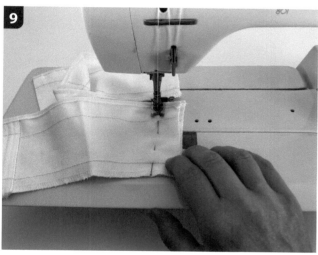

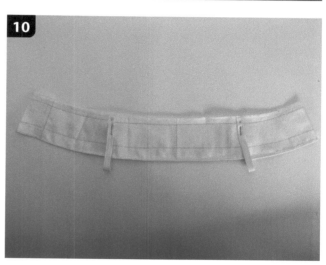

Waistband

STEP 1: The length of the waistband will have been determined at the fitting. In order to make it more comfortable, the following calculation will enable elasticated sections to be added at the sides without affecting the finished length. On 2.5cm-wide Petersham ribbon use a pencil to mark a dot 4cm from the raw edge. This dot is the CB and will eventually become the side without the extension. Next use the waist measurement from the fitting and, measuring from the first dot, mark the waist length, then a further mark 5cm away for the extension, followed by a final 6cm, cutting the Petersham at this point. The finished length should therefore be: the waistband measurement + 15cm (4cm + 5cm + 6cm). Locate the CF by marrying the CBs together, mark the CF and then find the quarters by matching the CF and CBs, which will eventually pitch up on the side seam of the basque.

STEP 2: Cut two pieces of 2.5cm-wide elastic, each 7.5cm long. Place these centrally over the marked quarter and parallel to your waistband: this can be done by eye. Pin in place in the centre of the elastic. Now stitch each of the raw edges of the elastic to the waistband with about a 5mm allowance, backstitching for strength.

STEP 3: The Petersham ribbon can now be cut behind the elastic on the dot. Fold under the raw Petersham as far as you can, and pin in place. You are effectively making a waistband which is exactly the correct length, but has a little stretch in it.

STEP 4: Fold in the 4cm allowances on the CB hook side to the same side on which the elastic was placed, and then tuck under enough of the raw edge to make a square. Pin in place and use a small- to medium- length machine stitch to sew each of the six boxes around all four sides with an edge stitch. It is easier and neater to stitch over the initial stitching on the first side of the box instead of backstitching. As before, it is easier to construct this like bunting and snip apart later, especially during this process as the layers of ribbon and elastic are quite thick and the sudden difference in thickness can be too much for the tension on some sewing machines to manage. Thread-mark the CF and CB extension line with straight machine lines. The waistband is now complete and ready to add to the basque.

STEP 5: Start by pinning back the basque side seam allowances before you apply the waistband: as they are on the underside as you stitch and out of sight, they have a tendency to flip in the wrong direction.

STEP 6: Lay the basque on the table with the inside uppermost (the side where the seam allowances are not visible) and apply the lower edge of the neat side of the waistband (without the raw elastic edges) to the line you have stitched at the waist of the basque. Due to the extensions, this will only fit one way up – just ensure the CFs match up, and the elastics fall at the side seams. Pin at the CBs and CF only, noticing that the basque is a tiny bit longer than the Petersham.

STEP 7: Working with the pinned side facing up, sew with a medium-sized stitch, and exactly match the stitching line at the basque waist to the lower edge of the Petersham: this is the actual waistline; the rest of the ribbon sits above it. Edge-stitch the waistband smoothly onto the basque until you reach the elastic, then grip the CF and stretch the waistband to take up the excess fabric in the basque, then stitch over the elastic section and continue to the CF. You will notice that the section of drill on the side seam has become slightly puckered: this will allow the elastic to stretch in the completed costume. Stitch the second side in the same way. The fact that the elastic is stretched as it is stitched means you do not need to use a zigzag stitch, which is normally needed to sew fabric or sections that stretch.

STEP 8: If you have been commissioned to make a tutu, it is a good idea to add your own label at this point. If you are making a set of costumes, adding the dancer's name on a tape at this stage means you can machine-stitch this on and have a professional-looking garment. The CB extension is a good position for this; aim to stitch it on neatly on the inner side. A slightly shorter machine stitch should help you achieve this.

STEP 9: The label will be viewed every time the costume is worn and it gives a good impression if this is neat and visually clear.

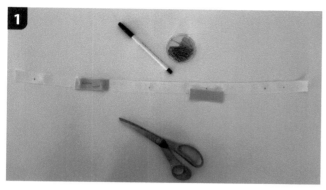

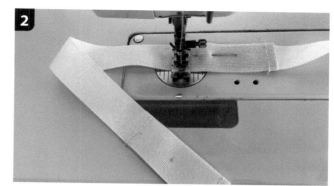

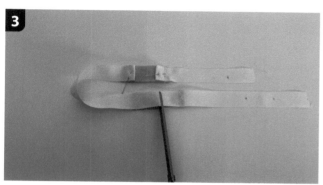

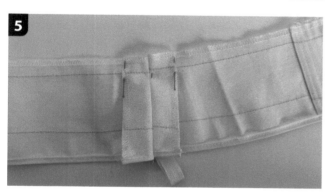

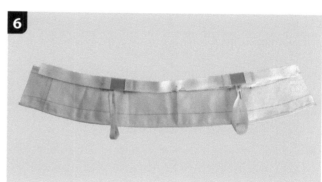

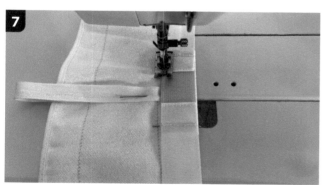

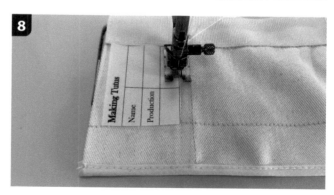

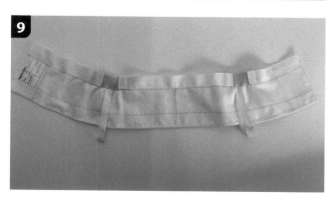

Waistband Fastenings

STEP 1: It is important that the waistband sits snuggly on the natural waist as it will prevent the finished costume moving up or down the body in wear. Use two corset hooks and eyes, stitched closely together within the 2.5cm-wide waistband. Although they may look quite large and bulky, unlike conventional hooks and bars, when stitched on correctly they won't accidently undo themselves in performance. Remember this waistband will be covered by the bodice so they will not be visible on the exterior when the costume is complete.

Stitch the hooks on by hand using a four-thread. Always set the position of the hooks first as they are located in a specific place; the eyes can be marked after this has been established. Place the head of the hook flat on the outside of the waistband, just back from the CB edge with the head curving out on the right-hand side. Remember to allow enough room for a second hook to nestle below it on the Petersham. The hook is positioned slightly away from the edge as it will be under some tension when done up and it shouldn't be allowed to 'travel' beyond the CB.

To sew on the hook, hide the knot of the four-thread within the finished edge of the waistband, then use stab stitches through one of the loops, ensuring you go all the way through the waistband and make neat prick stitches on the inside. Three stitches will provide strength and security. Repeat through the other loop, then pass the thread between the Petersham layers to the head. Put two stitches through each side to prevent the head from shifting around, before neatly fastening off with three small stitches. Stitch on the second hook.

STEP 2: To stitch on the eyes, line up the CBs. Take the eye element and place it over the hook so that it is again curving away from the Petersham. Mark its position on the extension side lightly in pencil, ensuring it is under tension similar to what it will experience when closed and on the body. Unhook and stitch in position – three stitches through each loop and then two over the 'neck' to allow access for the hook. Fasten off with three small stitches.

STEP 3: The knicker and basque sections are now complete and the tutu nets can now be assembled in preparation for construction.

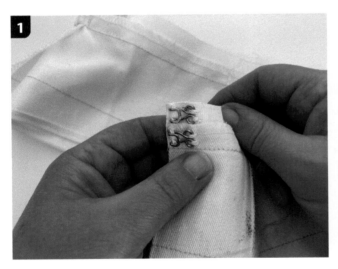

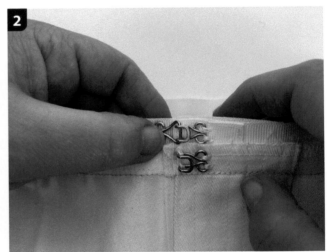

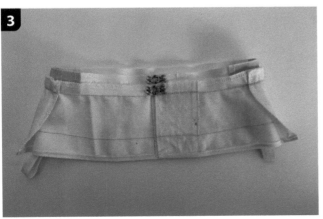

Preparing the net layers

STEP 1: Place the cut-out, edged and labelled net sections and in number order. Each separate layer will need to be stitched together into one long strip in preparation for the pleating stage. Start with the deepest high hip layer which contains the most widths. By starting with the layer which needs the most treatment, each subsequent layer will get quicker and easier. Set up the sewing machine with matching polyester thread and a medium-length straight stitch.

STEP 2: Remove the label from the uppermost layer and immediately repin to a single layer of the net. Remove the remaining pins from that layer.

STEP 3: The nets are joined into one length using an overlapped seam of about 7mm. For speed, arrange all the nets you are about to stitch together over one leg as you sit at the machine; they can then be kept in one place and are easy to add to the line. The seams do not need pinning, but start at the straight edge, not the edge with the points or scallops. If you are right-handed, overlay the right layer over the left layer and anchor them under the machine foot. Begin with a backstitch. Pull the under layer flat towards you as you gently place the upper layer on top and then guide both layers through the machine, stitching in the centre of the 7mm allowance.

STEP 4: Stitch as neatly as possible. Practice makes perfect, but be realistic: if you go slightly off, will it notice in the final garment? Probably not! Again, don't worry too much about having a whole point or scallop at the finished edge, but the apex of each shape should be level. Start and finish with a backstitch and make sure the tension is correct on your machine: the finished seam should sit flat and not be taut.

STEP 5: For speed, run each seam on from the previous one. As long as you do not join the end with the label attached to other sections, you will be in no danger of making a tube. When you have stitched together all the net sections needed for that layer, carry on stitching the other layers in number order until you reach Layer 1, then cut the threads to separate each layer into one long strip.

STEP 6: Include stitching the channel together into one long narrow strip in this process, but the leg ruffles can remain in two sections.

STEP 7: The nets will later be pleated to size, and in order to keep the tutu balanced, the net layers need to be divided into eighths which will match the eighths marked on the knicker. Take the longest layer and fold it in half, then into quarters, and finally into eighths. It is useful if you have someone to help you do this, or you could use the machine presser foot in the down position to lock the folds in place. Now cut a small notch or 'V' in the folded edges to make locating them simple. These notches will later be marked with a coloured thread as they are pleated. Leave the net layer folded and place to one side. Repeat with the remaining layers other than the channel strip and the leg frills, which do not need this treatment.

STEP 8: The channel strip needs to be added to the centre of the layer which has 'channel' marked on its label. It is important it is sewn on at an even distance from the edge; failure to do so will mean the hoop will sit crookedly. Either mark the position with a vanishing marker pen, or measure the distance from the edge of the table and place masking tape along this line. Place the long edge of the net against this and pin the channel in place. Stitch in place by sewing down each side of the strip, close enough to the cut edge to allow for easy access for the hoop that will eventually be threaded through, but not so close that the stitching line misses the channel edge and leaves gaps through which the hoop can escape.

STEP 9: It is easier to stitch the second edge with the strip underneath, as this avoids it 'chasing' – this is where the top layer of net pushes ahead of the lower layer and the two do not sit flat together.

STEP 10: With this process complete and the channel layer put back in order with other layers, they are now ready for pleating to the required length in preparation for adding to the knicker.

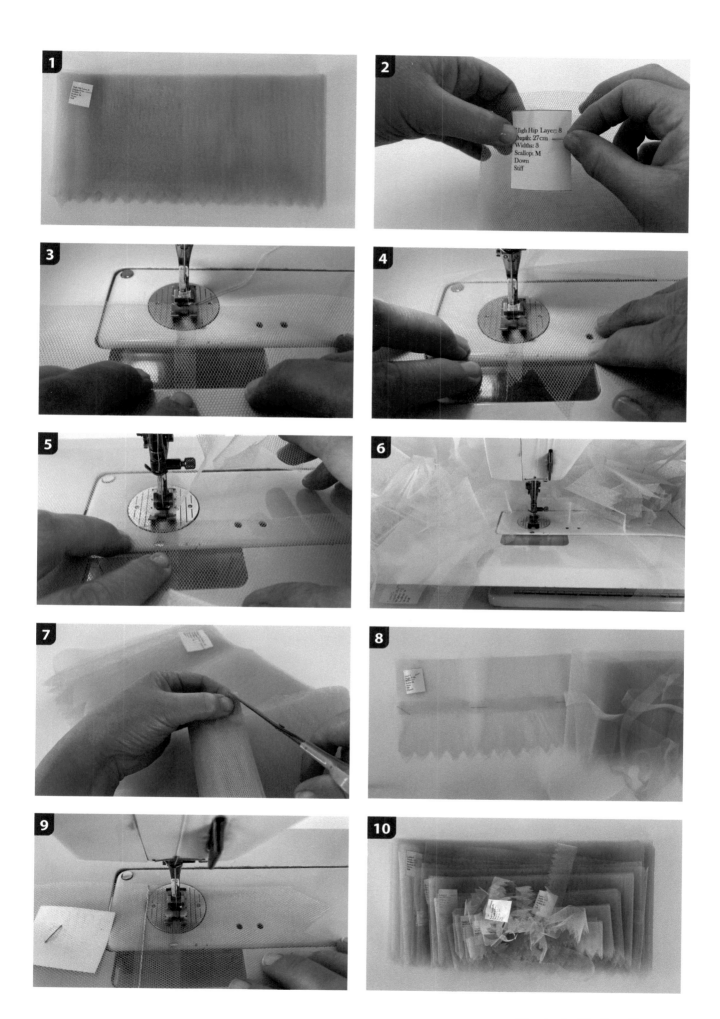

Pleating

Creating standard knife pleats by machine is a technique that most people can pick up quite quickly, but it requires some practice. It is much easier and more accurate to machine-pleat the nets rather than gathering them; although gathering may appear quicker initially, it is less easy to make sure the net is evenly distributed and there is always the danger that the thread can snap. A pleated treatment also means the head of the pleat is much flatter and will stitch neatly to the knicker.

Some tutu-makers prefer to use a pleating or ruffling attachment on their machine to reduce the net – I have not had much success with these as the quantities in each layer vary so much and so it needs constant adjustment. I find it quicker and more accurate to pleat by hand, but do give it a try if you're interested as it may work for you.

Begin with a practice session using a strip of spare net. Set the machine up with polyester thread and a straight stitch with a short stitch length; this will help you to have more control while you are learning, so the machine does not run away with you. Once you have mastered the technique, you should be able to keep your foot lightly on the foot pedal and pleat in one smooth action.

Use the edge of the foot as a guide and run the top edge of the net along it to make a consistent narrow heading about 7mm wide. It is this stitching line that will be followed when applying the layer to the line on the knicker.

STEP 1: The first set of pleating to practice is similar to a conventional knife pleat and has a ratio of 3:1. This uses three units of flat fabric to produce one unit of pleated fabric, immaterial of its width; making bigger pleats will not reduce the final length of the layer, which will remain exactly the same. Aim for the pleats to be around 7mm wide, so 21mm of fabric will be needed to create one pleat.

STEP 2: I like to use an awl to help guide the fold into the machine as it sits comfortably in the hand, but you could try a long, glass-headed pin or small pair of scissors. Some people prefer to use their fingers. Begin by folding the first pleat by hand and put it under the machine presser foot.

STEP 3: Put the awl or pin head at around 21mm from the fold of the first pleat and use it to guide the fabric underneath to make the second pleat.

STEP 4: Stitch and repeat, aiming to make 7mm pleats with no gaps between them, and nothing overlapping.

Put a piece of masking tape over the footplate of the machine if you are concerned about scratching it. Practise until you are happy with the technique. It does not need to be absolutely perfect: if your pleating 'handwriting' gives slightly larger pleats, that will be fine. The important thing is that the finished length will fit onto the knicker.

Unlike joining the nets together, where the labour-intensive top layers were completed first, I would recommend starting with the smallest leg ruffles to get into your rhythm. You will notice that the leg ruffle contains 3m of fabric, so this gets pleated down in a ratio of 3:1 to around 1m.

Follow on with Layer 1. If you measure the Layer 1 line on the knicker pattern, you will notice the distance is about a third of the length of the net, so pleat Layer 1 in exactly the same way as the leg ruffle with a 3:1 pleat. When you have finished it, check half the length of it against the pattern (which is itself half a knicker); ideally, the net should be about 2–3cm longer than the line onto which it will be stitched. Accuracy at this point will help with assembly and a good-quality outcome. Although it is possible to snip the odd thread to release the pleats in the event that the layer is too short, which would constrict the knicker if left as it is, this should be avoided if possible.

The recipe for the lower layers has been created by measuring the length of the layer on the knicker pattern, multiplying by three and adding a little if the sum does not equal a quarter of the net width. Layer 2 contains 2.25 layers, that is about 35cm longer than Layer 1. This amount is negligible, and if your Layer 1 was the correct final length, Layer 2 should be similar.

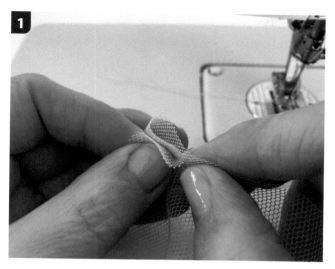

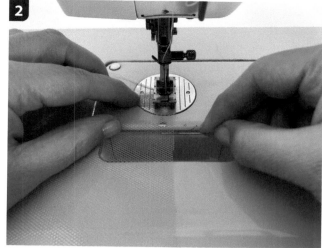

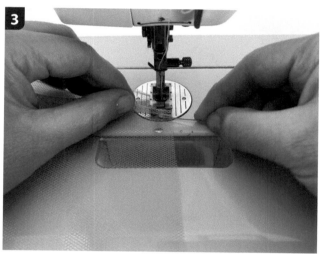

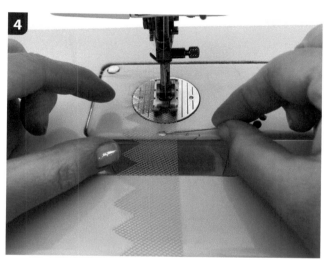

Handy tools to help with pleating

Embroidery scissors can be used to help pleat the net.

An awl can be a useful tool to aid with pleating as it sits well in the hand. Choose the tool that works best for you.

STEP 1: From now on mark each notch with a length of contrasting coloured thread. These thread-markers can be created by wrapping your hand with spare thread – I use old bobbin thread rather than throwing it away. The threads can then be snipped at two points to create a batch of thread-markers around 8cm long.

STEP 2: Use masking tape to stick these to the top of the sewing machine so they are easily accessible.

STEP 3: Whenever you come to a notch, simply lay the thread over the notch and keep sewing. Don't worry if you forget one or two or they drop out; you will have enough to act as a guide. As you finish each layer, neatly roll them up separately and safety-pin them to keep them in order with the label clearly visible.

STEP 4: Continue pleating with Layer 3. You will soon find you need to add in extra pleats; ideally this will be done regularly by overlapping the folded edges, but you can do this by adding a double pleat, then a single pleat, double, then single and so on. Soon you will need to build up the density with each subsequent layer. You make a double pleat by simply pleating on top of the first one, adding double the amount of fabric into the same width pleat.

STEP 5: Everyone pleats differently; you will find you have a sort of pleating 'handwriting'. You should pleat each layer in order, as only you can gauge the density from the previous layer. By the time you get to the top layer, you may be creating triple or even quadruple pleats. Just be sure to keep them a consistent width. I like to keep the pleats to about 7mm, as it gives a neat finish when you come to string them together, but use your judgement on this and make them larger if it suits your purpose.

If you find it impossible to stitch a precise distance from the straight edge, go back afterwards and stitch a second line of exact stitching; this is very useful as a guide for accurately stitching the net to the knicker. Equally, if you find the layer hasn't pleated up sufficiently, restitch by bunching it up or adding extra pleats as you go. Don't worry about removing the first stitch line as it will never show.

Other types of pleating

I have seen different types of pleating used on the high hip layer. Although the following two methods may initially seem complex, the net in the outer finished layer is naturally more evenly distributed. Depending on the density of the net, it can also look more structured and give a more pleasing visual effect.

Reverse pleating
The first stage of the pleat is similar to making a conventional knife pleat, but make it twice the size of regular tutu pleats at about 14mm. This pleat is then folded back on itself to create a 5:1 pleat: five units of fabric to one unit of pleat, which in this case would result with a pleat 7mm wide.

Fork pleating
STEP 1: This involves using a fork or a similar tool. Insert the tine nearest to you, and then fold the net underneath twice. This again reduces the quantity at 5:1; if even greater reduction is necessary, the pleats can be encouraged to sit on top of one another.

STEP 2: Experiment with different width forks to get the effect you are after. It may be worth adapting a plastic or wooden fork. It's the central gap which dictates the width of the pleat, so if necessary, create something that works for you by cutting out the central tines, and shortening the handle if it gets in the way when machining.

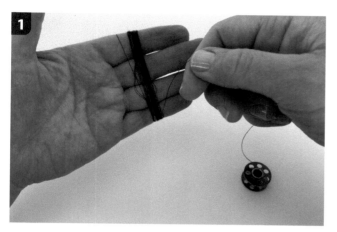

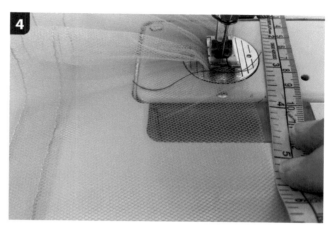

Fork pleating

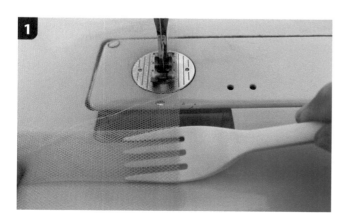

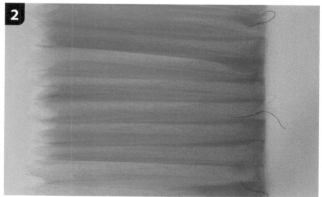

Assembling the tutu plate

All the component parts are now ready to start assembling the tutu plate: the basque, the flat knicker section and the pleated net layers.

The natural tendency of a net tutu is to want to drop with gravity. In order to mitigate this problem, the first few layers will be sewn on with the scalloped or pointed finished edge facing upwards in order to provide extra lift. Locate the leg ruffle and Layers 1, 2, 3 and 4 if you are making the larger sizes as you will need these first.

STEP 1: Begin by placing the knicker flat on the table. Use glass-headed pins to pin the stitch line on the pleated net Layer 4 to the thread-marked stitching line on the knicker located at the bottom of the opening. Remember to direct the pointed edge up towards the high hip line. Place pins at the CBs, then locate the coloured thread at the CF and pin to the CF junction on the knicker. Distribute the remaining net using the coloured threads as a guide.

If you have pleated accurately, you shouldn't need more than three pins here. If the layer is a little long, you can concertina the pleats together. In the event the layer is short or would need stretching in order to make it reach the CB, snip a couple of pleats to release them. This is not ideal practice, but if the layers are too short and not adjusted, the knicker will end up smaller than expected. It will be very difficult to resolve this at a later stage.

STEP 2: Machine-stitch the layers using polyester thread and a slight zigzag stitch. Test the stitch on a scrap of double bobbinet. The synthetic thread has some give in it, but make sure the stitch does not snap when stretched. It is likely that you will need to adjust the stitch several times until you reach the ideal length and width – do not to make the stitch length smaller than it needs to be in case it ever needs unpicking.

Stitch on this first layer, exactly matching the stitching line on the net pleats to the thread-marked line on the knicker. Ensure this and every other layer starts and stops exactly at the CB edge with an anchoring back-stitch. If you stop short there will be a bald section at the back, and if you extend the line it will get in the way of the French seam when you later come to join it. Remove the coloured thread-markers as you go; they are much easier to take out at this stage rather than after the tutu is complete. You will soon realise that the tutu in this stage will collect all manner of threads in the nets, so discard the thread-markers in a bin.

STEP 3: Now repeat the process with the next layer down, starting at the CBs and matching the pleated stitch line to the carbon paper line on the bobbinet. This can sometimes be difficult to see, so try adjusting your machine light or even turning it off; sometimes a less focused light can make it easier to locate. If it's still a problem, redraw the line with a vanishing marker or friction pen.

The traced lines are closest together at the front hip where the leg will swing forward; be careful to avoid catching the previous layer when you stitch on the next one or the plate will become lumpy and stiff.

Carry on adding the layers ending with Layer 1.

STEP 4: Now stitch on the leg ruffle, starting at the marked CB crotch line and continuing along the inner side of the bias binding, to the CF crotch line, making sure you do not encroach into the elastic channel; repeat on the other leg. These nets can be quite scratchy on the dancer's legs, so make sure the points are directed up the body as with the other layers. Attempt to do this without pinning as it will help with speed, but you must also ensure that the frill does not tighten up the knicker leg, this is the job of the elastic which will be added later. It is likely there will be an excess of leg ruffle and this can just be cut to size as needed.

STEP 5: Prepare the knicker to attach the remaining upper layers. The initial nets have been stitched on in one direction, and the remaining will be stitched in the opposite direction, so pin the CF seam in place on the underside so there is no confusion as to which way this seam falls.

STEP 6: Lay the knicker flat on the table and pin the stitched net layers out of the way to reveal the remaining traced lines. Use glass-headed pins and try to get some tension in the bobbinet to create a 'hump' with the already stitched net layers. Be aware that the more layers you stitch on, the more likely you are to catch the bobbinet knicker in a pleat underneath. This method of pinning the layers already attached out of the way should help you avoid this.

Now stitch on the remaining nets starting with the next layer above the opening – Layer 4 for the smallest size or Layer 5 for the others – this time with the points or scallops directed down the knicker. If using a domestic machine, it may be easier to remove the table and make use of the free arm. Carry on adding the layers sequentially. They shouldn't need additional pinning down other than the layer that is being worked on; it

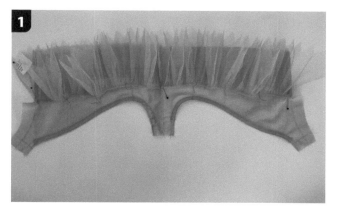

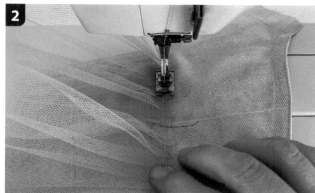

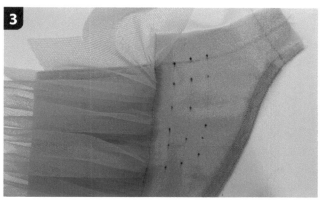

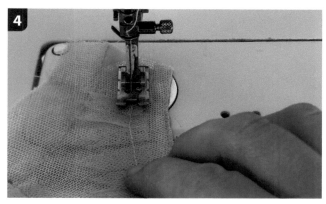

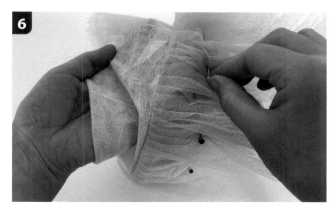

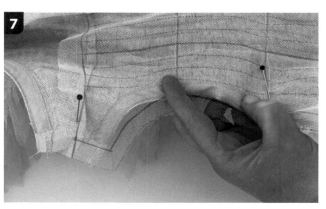

should be fine to let the layers sit where they choose without additional control. When the channel layer is reached, the channel can lie either way up: this won't affect the way the hoop sits.

STEP 7: It is important to sew precisely on the marked lines, paying special attention to stitching the final, uppermost layer accurately onto the high hip line. By this point it will be evident why excess bobbinet has been left to make stitching on these last layers easier.

When all the nets have been attached, double-check the knicker hasn't change size by laying the pattern against it. Remove all the pins and trim any thread ends. By this stage, you will be able to see the tutu starting to take shape.

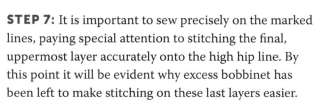

Joining the knicker centre back seams

STEP 1: Now the knicker section is ready to be completed. Join the knicker CBs together below the opening with a French seam. Begin by first pinning the lower net layers out of the way so there is no danger of trapping them in the seam.

STEP 2: With wrong sides together, pin the finished CB edge together, carefully matching the base of the opening and the crotch line.

STEP 3: Machine from the opening to the crotch using the pinned line as a guide for the edge of the foot as before. These last stages require firm handling of the now wayward layers of net. It is easier to sew in this direction, from the tricky opening where there are many layers towards the crotch.

STEP 4: Trim back the seam to 3mm outside the stitched line of the seam allowance. Finger-press this seam rather than trying to use an iron, and then pin the second line exactly on the CB before stitching, again from the opening to the crotch. The junction at the base of the opening is quite vulnerable, so make sure you catch in all the layers of bobbinet and encroach slightly into the turned-back area above the zig-zagged reinforcement. This will be restitched by hand afterwards.

STEP 5: The final task on the knicker is to French seam the crotch seam. Ensure the CF seam and CB seam allowances are pressed in opposite directions so they sit as flat as possible. Be careful not to stitch across the opening of the bias elastic channel as this will hamper adding the knicker elastic. This final French seam can be wider than the others to allow for future alteration.

Joining the centre back nets

STEP 1: The individual net layers now need linking together at the CB. This is not an easy task, so turn the tutu upside down and with the bulk of the tutu squashed beneath the table, seam the layers together as before using an overlapped seam and starting at Layer 1. Something to watch out for here is that you don't mix up the layers when joining them, so that for instance Layer 4 isn't accidently joined to Layer 5. Check twice before stitching.

Do not cut the threads between each layer until the end as they have a tendency to catch on the net points and unthread the machine. Carry on stitching layers together all the way from the outside edge to the CB seam until the base of the knicker opening has been reached.

STEP 2: From this layer upwards, account needs to be taken of the CB opening to ensure the dancer still has space to get into the costume. Leave the distance from where that layer joins at the CB to the bottom of the opening plus 3cm for ease. Mark with a glass-headed pin at that point. Then starting at the outside edge, stitch the nets together with an overlapped seam until you reach this pin, and then backstitch.

Do not stitch the channel layer together, or you will not be able to access it to add the hoop. When all the remaining layers have been joined, remove from the machine, and trim back and discard all the thread ends.

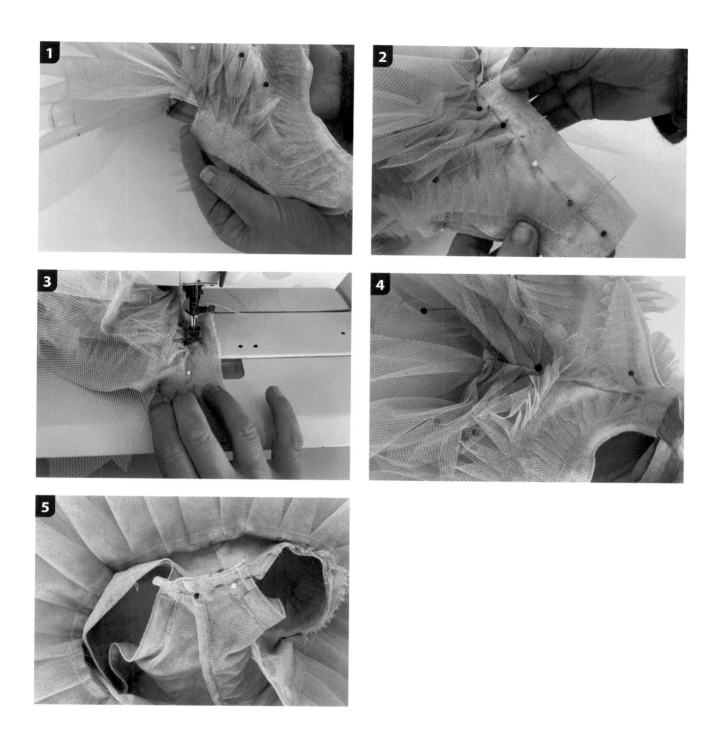

Joining the centre back nets

Completing the knicker

STEP 1: Reinforce the vulnerable area at the base of the CB opening by hand-stitching a piece of cotton tape across it on the inside.

STEP 2: Elasticate the knicker legs by first measuring the length of the bias channel on the pattern and subtracting 2cm from this measurement. Cut two lengths of 5mm elastic and insert into each bias channel using small safety pins. Overlap the ends by about 2cm and hand-sew closed with a double thread. The elastic can be adjusted after the fitting if necessary.

A hook and eye can also be added to the inside of the CB to the hoop layer. My experience of working in a department where many different dancers wear the same tutu means it can be useful to put more hooks down the centre back especially if the tutu knicker is tight. Generally, with a properly fitted tutu this shouldn't be necessary.

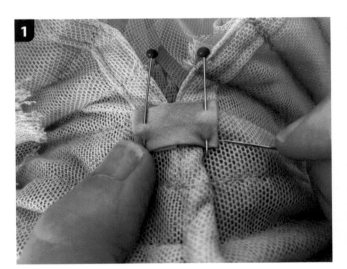

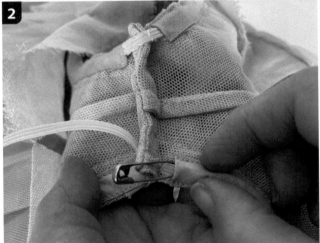

Joining the basque to the tutu

STEP 1: The basque needs pinning to the inside of the knicker. Remember the hanging loops sit on the inside of the basque. Take a pin and stab through the knicker at the junction of the high hip and CF seam and then the CF on the high hip line of the basque.

STEP 2: Use a second pin to join them horizontally along the high hip line. This prevents the two points from slipping against each other so they will be held together accurately.

STEP 3: Next, pin the CBs.

STEP 4: Don't forget you have an extension on the left-hand side of the basque, but nothing on the right-hand side of the basque or the knicker opening.

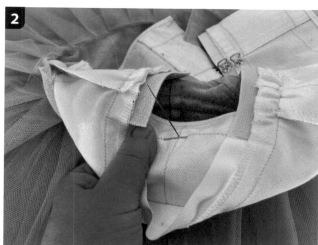

STEP 5: Distribute the rest of the knicker around the high hip line – the quarter mark on the bobbinet should correspond with the side seam, but don't force it if it sits better elsewhere. Just make sure the knicker is evenly distributed on both sides. The bobbinet knicker should be a little bigger than the high hip line on the basque – it should never be tight.

STEP 6: Stitch the knicker and basque together with a cotton four-thread. Accurately sew them together along the high hip line working from the inside. Start by hiding the knot within the net as knots on the inside can rub against the dancer's skin and become uncomfortable.

STEP 7: Use a backstitch, with around a 6mm stitch on the inside and a 12mm stitch on the net outside. Due to the tough nature of the layers of fabric, the cotton thread is especially vulnerable at the eye of the needle and pulling it through several times can lead to it shearing. To help alleviate this, run a little beeswax along the four-thread to help stop it twisting and to give it a little more longevity.

STEP 8: This is an important row of stitching for the construction of your costume, and it needs to be sewn strongly. After you have done around 10cm, check the tension by trying to pull the tutu knicker away from the basque – is should be quite snug, with no gaps, but not too tight either or the costume could end up too small. Continue backstitching all the way around to the CB and fasten off strongly with a few small stitches, keeping all the finishing stitches to the outside to keep the side that touches the dancer as smooth as possible.

Some tutu-makers like to connect the basque to the tutu by machine, but I find it too much of a fight, and hard to get accurate. But by all means give it a go to see if it suits you.

STEP 9: Trim back any excess bobbinet to 1.5cm.

STEP 10: Stitch a size 3 dress hook and eye to close the basque at the CB high hip line.

STEP 11: The hook should go on the inside of the basque so it is invisible when done up, and the bar should go over the net at the CB.

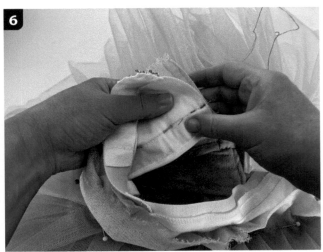

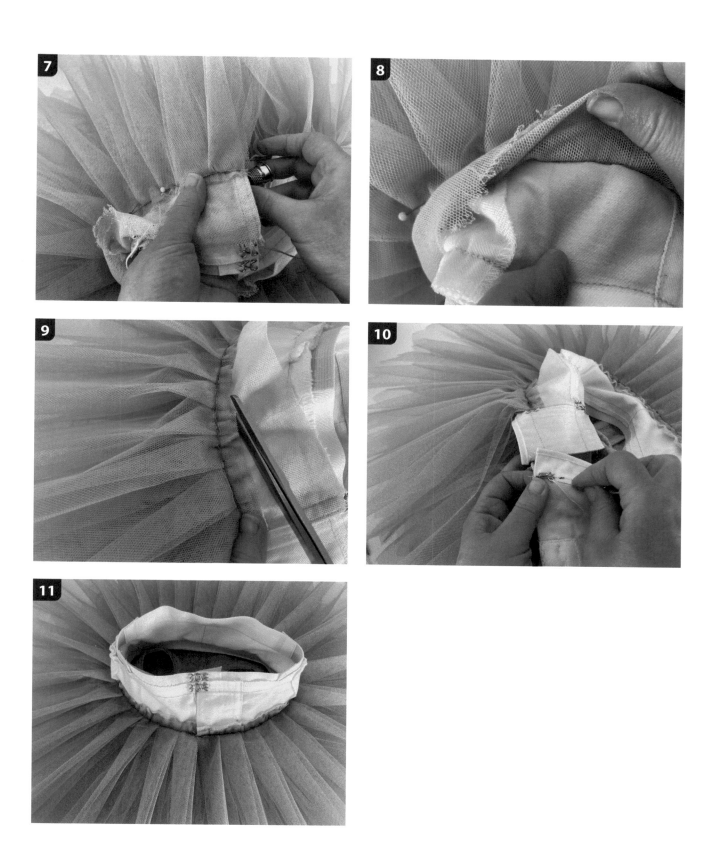

Adding the hoop

STEP 1: To add the hoop, close all the fastenings on the basque and turn the tutu upside down. Close the CB opening on the channel level using either the hook and eye if using or a safety pin if not.

STEP 2: To keep the lower levels below the channel level out of the way, use a length of elastic to tie them together like a ponytail.

STEP 3: A tutu for a professional dancer needs a 7mm steel hoop. If the tutu is for another purpose, a plastic hoop will suffice. Depending on the density of the plastic, you may need to use it double to provide support.

Push one end of the boning into the gap with a safety pin at its head; wrap masking tape around the junction between the pin and the boning.

STEP 4: Begin to thread the hoop through the channel from CB to CB, adjusting as you go so that the gathered net is evenly distributed.

There is a knack to this and the smooth edges of the safety pin should ease the insertion, stopping the boning corners from getting caught in the holes of the net. Once a length of around 50cm has been inserted, push the net along the boning and adjust the pleats, then repeat until the safety pin and boning emerge from the other side of the channel.

STEP 5: Aim to thread as much boning into the channel as possible without the tutu plate distorting.

STEP 6: If the tutu takes on a taco shape, there is too much boning so adjust accordingly. If the tutu looks smaller than it should and a bit constricted, add in a little more boning. The final decision on the hoop length doesn't need to be made until after the fitting, so leave the ends uncut for now while you arrange the pleating.

STEP 7: Locate the knicker CF seam and with the tutu still upside down, place it on the table with the CF seam facing away from you.

STEP 8: Start by leaning over the tutu and making sure the net is radiating out from this CF point in a straight line by pulling the net from the outside edge. This will help the hoop to sit flatter within the channel. Next check the side seams or quarters, and again pull the net pleats so they begin to fan out from the knicker like the spokes of a wheel.

STEP 9: Carry on this process until you reach the CB before reviewing the shape. If you are after a plate or pancake tutu, thread as much boning as possible into the channel without it distorting the knicker – you need to get it to the point where adding even a little bit more will cause it to warp. If the eventual tutu shape you are after is a drop or bell tutu, the hoop needs to be a little smaller so the upper net layers can fall over it.

STEP 10: When you are happy with the way the tutu is sitting, mark this junction where the boning meets with a pencil. Leave 10cm or so extra allowance and then cut the plastic boning with scissors.

STEP 11: My preference when using steel boning is to use the fold and snap method as the corners remain very sharp. If each end has been treated in this manner, it is possible to make the sharp edges rest into each other, rather than facing out and risking a nasty scratch to the dancer or her partner.

Use two pieces of masking tape to close the ring in order to check it is the correct length at the second fitting before finishing it properly. Now remove the safety pin at the CB knicker. The tutu should retain its shape and the CB should remain closed.

Steel boning generally comes in white, and covered either with plastic or fabric, as does the plastic version. If you are making a coloured tutu you may need to spray-paint the hoop or cover it with matching bias to stop it showing in the finished plate.

Finishing the steel boning to avoid scratches.

Setting the tutu plate

The net layers now need organising and steaming into shape before they are stitched together.

STEP 1: With the inner layers of the tutu still retained by the elastic tie used when inserting the hoop, ensure the tutu is closed at the high hip and lay the tutu flat on its back on the table. Fill the iron with water in preparation to steam each layer. Begin with the channel layer, holding the outer net edge in your left hand and push steam into the layer moving from where it joins to the knicker towards the outer edge, evening out any pleats which appear disorganised or are not radiating out from the centre as you go.

STEP 2: This steaming process should have quite a dramatic effect and this layer will look much more structured when it is finished. Release the next layer from the elastic bunch and let it settle on top of the hoop layer. As before, hold the outside edge in your left hand, organising and levelling out any wayward pleat, before applying steam to the heading and moving out to the edge.

STEP 3: Carry on with this process, separately steaming each layer until the leg ruffles are reached.

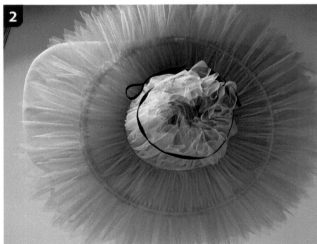

Stringing

During the stringing process, the layers of the tutu are stitched together. Stringing is a vital part of finishing your tutu: it keeps the layers together in movement and helps the tutu to retain its shape.

You will need to refer to the information in the stringing table, which differs according to the number of layers in the plate and whether a pancake or drop plate is desired. Take a set of upholstery or saddler needles; these are especially long, straight needles, and although not essential, are ideal for the purpose. I have a set of twelve, and I would recommend this number of needles as it

enables you to insert several strings before tying them off, which adds to the accuracy and speed of the process.

Load the needles with cotton four-threads in a colour that matches the net layers. These threads can be longer than are used for hand-sewing, so cut around 2.5–3m thread, post both ends through the eye and line up the halfway point and the cut ends. No knots are needed, and the needles should be neatly lined up in a pin cushion or similar where they will be less likely to become entangled.

If the tutu has graded colours, match the thread colour to the area you are stringing. This may mean several different coloured strings are added to the same plate.

Stringing table for pancake tutus

Child – 8-layer tutu	Ring 1	Ring 2	Ring 3	Ring 4	Topskirt
Layers	1–4	3–6	5–8	N/A	8–T
Length of string	5cm/2in	3cm/1in	1.5cm/½in	N/A	1.5cm/½in
Distance apart	5cm/2in	10cm/4in	10cm/4in	N/A	10cm/4in

Teen – 10-layer tutu	Ring 1	Ring 2	Ring 3	Ring 4	Topskirt
Layers	1–3	3–8	5–10	9–10	10–T
Length of string	5cm/2in	3cm/1in	2cm/¾in	1.5cm/½in	1.5cm/½in
Distance apart	5cm/2in	10cm/4in	10cm/4in	10cm/4in	10cm/4in

Adult – 12-layer tutu	Ring 1	Ring 2	Ring 3	Ring 4	Topskirt
Layers	1–5	4–9	6–12	11–12	12–T
Length of string	5cm/2in	5cm/2in	3cm/1in	1.5cm/½in	1.5cm/½in
Distance apart	5cm/2in	10cm/4in	10cm/4in	10cm/4in	10cm/4in

Stringing table for drop tutus

Child – 8-layer tutu	Ring 1	Ring 2	Ring 3	Ring 4	Topskirt
Layers	1–4	3–6	5–8	N/A	8–T
Length of string	5cm/2in	4cm/1½in	1.5cm/½in	N/A	1.5cm/½in
Distance apart	5cm/2in	10cm/4in	10cm/4in	N/A	10cm/4in

Teen – 10-layer tutu	Ring 1	Ring 2	Ring 3	Ring 4	Topskirt
Layers	1–3	3–8	5–10	9–10	10–T
Length of string	5cm/2in	8cm/3in	8cm/3in	1.5cm/½in	1.5cm/½in
Distance apart	5cm/2in	10cm/4in	10cm/4in	10cm/4in	10cm/4in

Adult – 12-layer tutu	Ring 1	Ring 2	Ring 3	Ring 4	Topskirt
Layers	1–5	4–9	6–12	11–12	12–T
Length of string	5cm/2in	7cm/2½in	8cm/3in	1.5cm/½in	1.5cm/½in
Distance apart	5cm/2in	10cm/4in	10cm/4in	10cm/4in	10cm/4in

STEP 1: With the tutu upside down, start by inserting the innermost row of strings. For the child's tutu, these strings link Layers 1–4, for the teen tutu they link Layers 1–4, and the for the adult tutu they link Layers 1–5. They are placed 5cm apart and are around 5cm in length for every size of tutu. A glance at the knicker pattern will show these layers differ the most in placement – they are all very close at the area either side of the CF near the hip bone, where the leg swings forward, and they open up as they reach the CB, over the buttocks, so we are starting with the most variable set of swing catches first.

STEP 2: Locate Layer 1 at the CB. Keeping hold of this point, find the remaining layers in Ring 1. Make a stab stitch straight down through all the layers, and straight back up again. Try not to pick up any pleated net, just single layers. The nature of the length of the nets at this point means the stitch may need to go in at an angle: when Layer 4 is reached (for the child or teen, Layer 5 for the adult), take a small stitch – no more than 5mm wide – and return to Layer 1. Leave the needle and ends hanging, and then put in your next stitch – about 5cm away from the first. Continue around the tutu linking all the nets in Ring 1 in a line radiating out from the tutu's centre until you have worked round the tutu.

STEP 3: These strings now need knotting off. Starting at the sides, stretch the knicker out as if it was being worn and note the length at which the thread should be knotted off while not constricting the layers. Try to economise on the length of thread used by pulling the needle and thread through the nets until there is about 12cm of thread left hanging in order to tie the knot. Leave another 12cm tail beyond the stringing stitch and cut the needle off at this point. There should still be plenty of thread in the needle for further strings.

STEP 4: Tie a thumb knot with the two ends and use a pin to guide the knot into exactly the right position.

STEP 5: Trim the ends neatly to around 7mm.

STEP 6: As you move around the tutu knotting off the strings on ring 1, you will notice they need to be longest at the CF and CB crotch, not only because of the position in which they are stitched onto the knicker, but also to account for the difference in length of each net layer – they may need to be longer by the time they get to the most exaggerated area over the bottom, and then shorter as they return to the side front.

When this first set of strings is complete, check the CF and CB area as they sometimes need an extra couple of stitches between the existing ones to give the nets more control. Use your judgement here. This first set of strings is the most complicated as they vary in length. The lengths of the strings on the remaining rings should be consistent.

STEP 7: With the first ring of strings in place, the tutu should be starting to take shape. Turn it the right way up. If you have a mannequin available in the correct size, put the tutu on it. It is important the mannequin is a similar size to the dancer, so pad out any areas to reflect this or you may end up with a distorted tutu. It is not essential to use a mannequin; stringing the remaining layers can be done on a flat surface. Without a dancer inside it, the shape of the basque will become rounder than it will be in wear. To imitate the dimensions of the dancer link the CF to the CB at the high hip on the basque with a piece of tape. This should be around 15cm on a child, 17.5cm on a teen and 20cm on an adult. For a plate or pancake tutu plate, tie the layers above the already steamed hoop layer out of the way with elastic.

The method for making both styles of tutu is the same until this point, but now you will need to follow the instructions for the shape of tutu you wish to create. There will always be a ring of strings within the hoop, and then one which sits outside the hoop. The top couple of layers will also be caught together at the outside edge with shorter strings, and a further row of strings is needed if a top skirt is added.

The tutu shapes differ in the hoop length, the steaming technique and the length of strings used.

Be aware throughout this process that if you plan to add a top skirt its weight will have an impact on the finished shape, unless it is a single layer of net. In this case it is better for the plate to look 'perkier' at this stage as it is likely to settle over time.

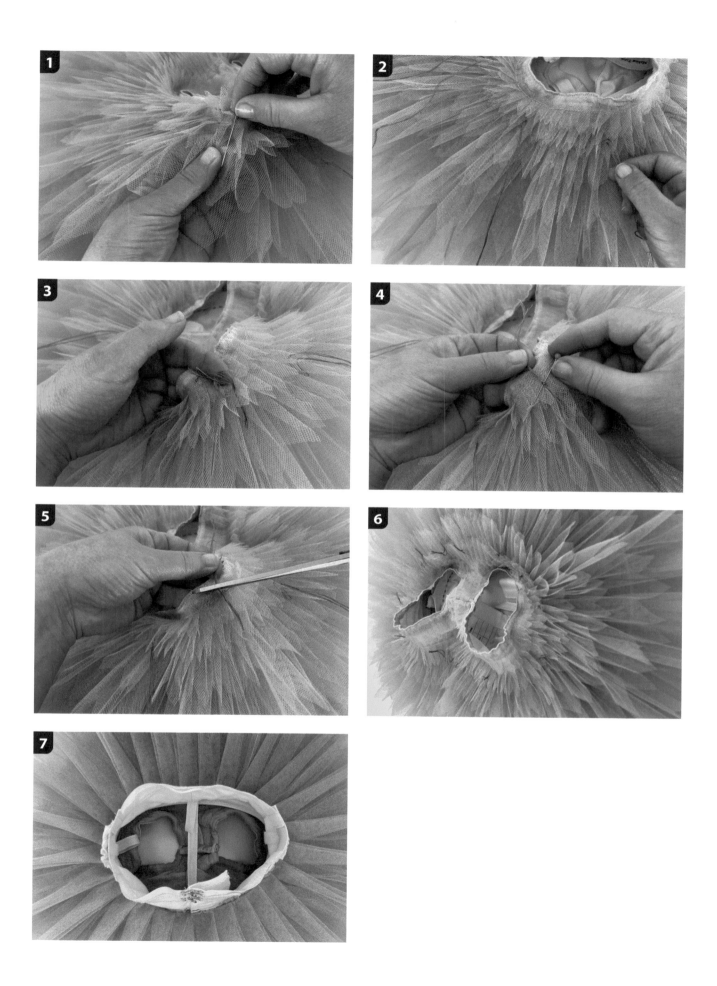

Plate or pancake tutu

Check the hoop – does it sit flat and provide a structure to which you can stitch the remaining layers of net? It should feel taut within the channel as though not a single extra centimetre can be added without it distorting. Adjust its length at this stage if necessary by retaping the hoop at the CB.

STEP 1: Release the next layer above the hoop and use the steam iron to give a light steam and settle any pleats into place – go around systematically checking for irregular or bulky net areas, arranging them as evenly as you can, as you did previously with the lower layers. When you are happy with how it looks, and there are no wayward-looking areas with everything flowing nicely from the bobbinet knicker, let another layer of net down and begin to steam as before. Without being tempted to over-steam at this stage, carry on until the top layer has been steamed and assess the shape.

STEP 2: If the tutu is as flat as required, use glass-headed pins to pin the outside layers into place, grabbing several layers of net at a time. If you want to exaggerate the pancake shape, it is possible to slightly pull the top layer before pinning. Gravity will mean that the nets want to drop over time, so encouraging them to do the opposite will help the tutu to retain its shape.

Drop tutu

STEP 1: For a drop tutu plate, either place the tutu on a mannequin or find a small cushion or folded towel and mould to a size into which the tutu crotch and basque can sit. This will provide some depth to encourage the softer bell shape. Tie the layers above the already steamed hoop layer out of the way with elastic.

Have a look at the hoop; you may judge it is too big and hindering the drop shape. If this is so, reduce its length by adjusting it at the CB and retaping. Be aware that shortening the hoop length by only 3cm can have a quite dramatic effect on the shape, so it may only need a small adjustment which will get checked at the second fitting. Systematically give each layer a light steam and evenly settle any pleats into position, gently placing the layers over the hoop.

STEP 2: When you have finished steaming the final layer, assess the shape. The drop shape can be exaggerated by pinning the outer edge while encouraging the upper layers back slightly, unlike the plate tutu where you pull the upper layers taut.

Completing the stringing

STEP 1: Remove the tutu plate from the mannequin and flip it onto its back in preparation for adding the second ring of strings, which when finished will provide even more structure to the finished plate.

It is important the remaining stitches are staggered – if you always put one at the CB and CF, you will start to create ridges or furrows, so start at a random position each time.

In all sizes this second ring stitching will connect further lower layers and pitch up inside the hoop. Refer to the stringing chart and locate the necessary layers. Stitch straight down from the underneath through the layers until you reach the hoop layer or the one after it, ensuring the nets are evenly distributed. Take a small stitch and return, as before try not to go through any net pleats, and repeat at around 10cm/4in intervals. Knot off this second ring of strings according to the chart, noting the length of these threads changes according to whether a plate or drop tutu is required.

STEP 2: The 10-layer and 12-layer tutus each require a fourth row of strings which sit outside the hoop and go all the way through to the high hip layer. Again, try not to catch pleats into the stringing stitch, and distribute any bulk as you come to it. These strings should be at around 10cm apart, remembering not to make their placement too regular to avoid creating furrows. Tie off according to the chart and trim back the ends to 7mm.

The final ring of strings links the upper layers and these can again be put in from the underside at 10cm gaps, but this time tie them off at a depth of 1.5cm.

Turn the tutu the correct way up and check the shape. In the past, the available net was much stiffer and we would often crush it into shape under a heavy board or even a mattress. Although this should not be necessary now, if you want a flatter plate tutu, this can be achieved by flipping it onto its back and leaving it under a weighted board for a day or so.

The plate tutu should be stored either flat or hung upside down with the hanging loops pulled through the knicker legs. The drop tutu can be hung the right way up in the short term or stored flat to avoid it dropping further.

The tutu plate is now complete and you can look forward to trying it on the dancer at the second fitting.

Plate or pancake tutu

Drop tutu

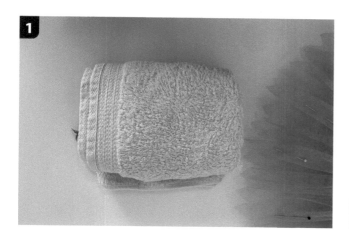

Completing the stringing

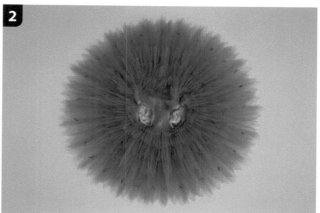

CHAPTER 4

The Bodice

Y ou can now make the bodice, knowing the trickiest processes of the costume are out of the way.

Cutting out the bodice and piping

The bodice backing

Costumes generally are not lined as this adds bulk, while also making them hard to launder and more labour-intensive to alter. Dance costumes in particular are subjected to sweat each time they are worn, so although not lined, the top fabric is backed onto a cotton fabric like a drill or coutil, which adds strength and body to the final garment as well as absorbing sweat.

The warp and weft should run perpendicular to each other in a high-quality fabric. Check this in the backing fabric by first making a small snip in the selvedge near the cut edge of the fabric and ripping along the weft. This tear should run the whole width of the cloth, so if you are left with a narrow triangle of cloth, make a further cut 2cm below the initial slash and repeat. You will need to repeat this process later when you come to cut out the top fabric, but if the fabric is delicate, pull one of the weft threads which will reveal the weave and enable you to cut along it accurately with scissors. Getting the correct grain is always very important when making a garment, and especially so when mounting two textiles together. Failure to do this can result in the grains distorting, so pay particular attention to it at this stage.

Once you have squared off the weft, in preparation for cutting out, fold the backing fabric in half selvedge to selvedge; does it fold happily in half, or does it swing off grain resulting in a visible triangle at one end? If this is the case grab hold of one corner and get a friend to hold the diagonal of the selvedge that needs realigning and pull back into shape. This takes quite a lot of strength, but refolding the fabric should reveal evidence of the weave having been reset to its original state. This process should be completed before pressing the fabric with a steam iron to make it as flat as possible; this is often more easily tackled when the cloth is slightly damp.

If you are using a backing fabric such as drill which has a different look on each side due to the weave, pick the side that you would prefer to be visible in the finished garment and fold it to the inside.

Just as for the toile, pin the altered bodice pattern onto the backing fabric with the CB and CF parallel to the selvedges and the waistline on the remaining pattern pieces at 90 degrees to the selvedge. Ensure there is sufficient space for the seam allowances, the same as when you cut out the toile: 11cm on the CBs, 4cm on the side seams, 4cm on the top or neckline edge, 2cm on the bottom edge and 2cm on the remaining bodice seams. As when pinning out the knicker and basque, use minimal pins and be mindful of not pinning over the pattern lines or waistline to make it easier when you come to trace out. If the bodice is likely to be altered many times in the future, leave extra length on the bottom edge to allow alteration for a dancer with a longer body length.

The top fabric

Is it obvious which is the right side of the fabric? If not, use whichever side you like best. Mark the wrong side in the selvedge by pencilling an arrow, pointing upwards, towards what will become the top of the garment. Mark arrows at intervals down the selvedges on both sides. The appearance of some fabrics like velvet can change in the light depending on which way up they are, so ensure all pattern pieces are placed in the same direction on the fabric.

Ideally you should cut the fabric in the same direction as you cut the drill, with the strongest warp threads running up and down each panel piece. However, if you have a fabric like a dupion which contains a slub, consider if you are happy for these obvious bumps to run around the body – you may instead want to cut it across the grain with the weft threads running up each panel.

The finished bodice will be piped top and bottom; if you have plenty of fabric, it is preferable to avoid seaming the bias strip as this eliminates bulk. Cut ample bias strips first, as it is time-consuming and frustrating to have to go back and make extra. You will be able to fit your bodice pattern sections into the remaining fabric and therefore use it as economically as possible. As a guide, 2.5m of bias strips should be plenty to pipe the top and bottom edge of the bodice.

STEP 1: Fold the selvedge to meet the weft thread and pin the folded edge. You ideally need this fold to be across the entire width of the fabric.

STEP 2: Mark a line 3.2cm from the fold, so you will effectively be cutting two strips out at once. Measure the length, and if necessary mark a second line so you have the required quantity. Cut along the marked lines and then splice down the fold. Ensure you have marked the wrong side of the fabric on each of these strips and set to one side.

STEP 3: Fold the top fabric in half, selvedge to selvedge, and place the drill bodice sections as efficiently as possible. It is important that the grain is accurate and exactly echoes that of the drill backing. If you are planning to use the same fabric to decorate the top skirt, ensure you are left with a large enough section; it may be necessary to mark out what you think you will need for the skirt on the fabric and then cut the bodice from what is left.

STEP 4: Cut out the bodice sections slightly larger than the backing. The top fabric will in effect be wrapped over the drill when it is on the body, and then again folded back on itself at the seamlines and again with the piped top and bottom edges. The top fabric therefore needs to be slightly bigger than the drill inner bodice or it will be too tight and the bodice will be smaller than required.

STEP 5: To achieve this, place the drill panel onto the fabric and align the grain. Put a pin into the centre of the waist. Using the heel of your hand as an anchor, push the drill away from you with your fingers and place another pin in the centre of the panel, about 7.5–10cm away from the first one. Continue until you reach the top line, then turn the piece around and push the fabric from the waist to the high hip line. Then repeat, this time pushing from the centre of the pattern piece to the marked lines.

STEP 6: Pin at 90 degrees to all the seam lines so you will be able to efficiently machine stitch straight over the pins. Continue pushing the cloth, radiating out from the original waist pin.

STEP 7: When you turn over the finished panel there should be a slight 'bubbling' – this is a good sign.

Fabrics with a pattern or stripe

If the fabric has a strong design, think about where it should be placed on each panel. Pay particular attention to the CF panel. If you are unsure, cut out a negative CF panel in paper on a fold, so you get the entire width of the CF, and then try it in different positions on the fabric to work out the best pattern placement. You may decide to take this approach to pattern placement on the CB too. If the top skirt will be in the same fabric, check there is enough to ensure effective pattern placement on the skirt before cutting out the smaller bodice sections and piping. If fabric quantity is tight, save cutting the piping until last, which may involve joining bias sections or making it in several small sections.

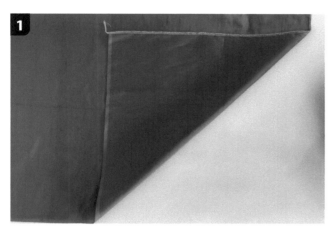

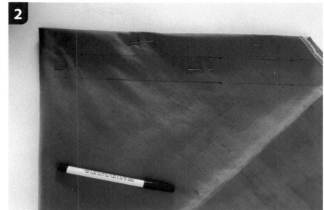

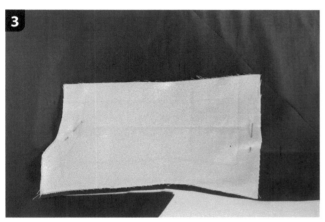

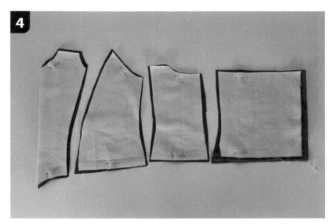

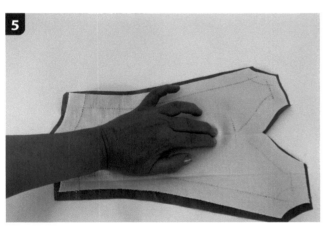

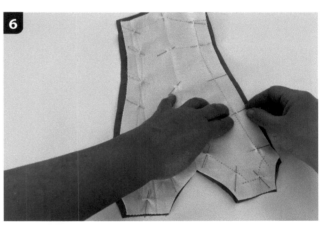

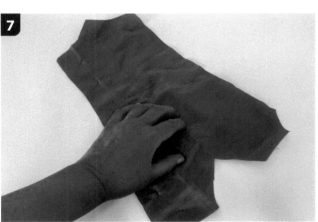

Save all scraps until the costume is finished; they are useful for checking stitch lengths and iron temperatures, and as colour samples.

Marking up and mounting

STEP 1: Trace the construction lines on the pattern pieces onto the bodice fabric pieces using dressmaker's carbon paper, as described in Chapter 2.

STEP 2: Use thread which matches your top fabric. Machine-stitch the vertical seam lines just outside the traced line using a long straight stitch from raw edge to raw edge. Find a place on your machine foot to use as a guide, and stitch a consistent distance from the marked seam line. Stitch both sides of a test panel and check the top fabric doesn't creep or pleat; if it does (and this can happen with fabrics like velvet), you will need to hand-tack the whole bodice. Remember, however, that the panel won't look perfectly flat as the pinning has added a little excess which will flatten out when the bodice is assembled.

STEP 3: If you are happy with the result of your test, the remaining sections can be stitched down the vertical seam lines. Do not backstitch the panels, and start and finish at the raw edge. Run one into the next without cutting the threads for efficiency. Leave the CB line free from stitching as this will need to be checked it is in the correct position at the second fitting; a machine-stitched line may leave a mark if it needs alteration.

The upper neck edges and lower high hip lines, waistlines and CB line all need hand-tacking. Take a contrast-coloured single thread and hand-tack using stitches about 2cm long. Try to make certain that the thread will show on the right side at the junctions when the bodice is assembled. You can now remove any remaining pins, and give each panel a gentle press.

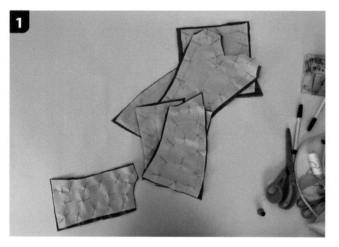

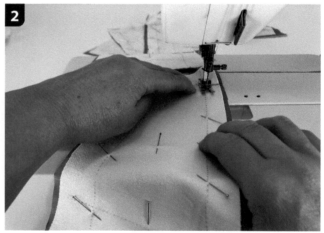

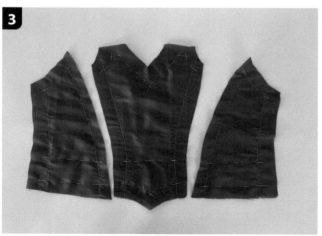

Finishing the raw edges

Overlocking or zigzagging the raw edges

STEP 1: Finish the vertical edges of the panels, which are unlikely to be altered in the second fitting, at this stage; it makes stitching the sections together and then pressing easier.

STEP 2: You will need to clip about 12mm of the seam at the waist and all the concave curves. This will allow you to counter-stretch them as you neaten the raw edges, so they will lie flat when pressed. If you have an overlocker, use the edge of the foot as a guide to run down the stitch line from the RS to leave a seam allowance of about 1.5cm. Leave the side seams, the CB top line and lower high hip sections unfinished until they have been checked.

STEP 3: If you don't possess an overlocker, use a long stitch and stitch about 1.5cm away from the seam line. Trim back neatly to the machine line.

STEP 4: Then sew using a medium to large zigzag stitch, ensuring the centre of the zigzag sits on the guide stitch line, the left side of the zigzag goes into the fabric and the right side zigzag goes over the guide line and off the raw edge so it binds the edge.

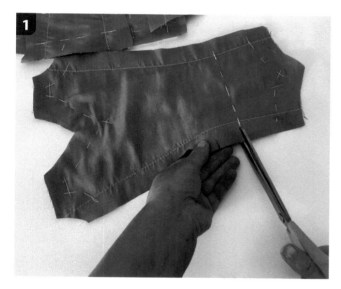
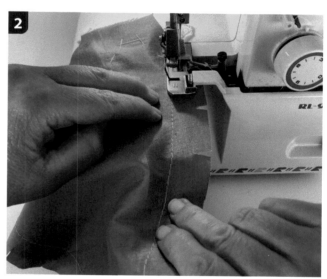
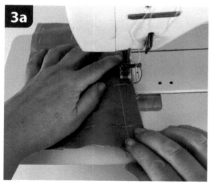
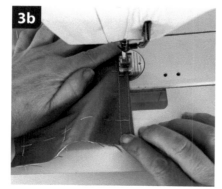
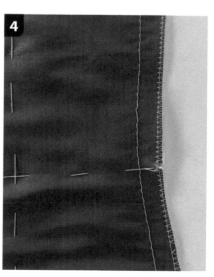

Assembly

If you stitch each of the panels together in the same direction, for instance in an upward direction from the high hip line towards the neckline, the machine foot has a tendency to push the upper panel forward, resulting in a tiny discrepancy over the length of the seam. Although this is not disastrous on one panel, a 2mm displacement on each seam will result in a twisted bodice; so when you join the completed bodice at the CB, the waistline could have shifted by 2cm or more.

Centre Front and Back Panels

Begin by pinning the following sections together in pairs: the two CF panels, the SF and SSF, and the CB/SB. For the child's seven-piece bodice, pin both SF sections to the CF in the same direction. Push a pin through the junction of the waist and the seam line and locate this point on the second piece. Next match the high hip and then the top line; as when pinning together the toile, the pattern pieces should fit together exactly with no ease. This is easiest to find after you have pinned it together by running your fingers along each side of the seam. In

the event the marking is not totally accurate, match the waist and release the seam above or below so it sits flat. Pin these four or five seams together in the same direction. When you come to connect the remaining seams, pin and stitch them in the reverse direction.

Thread up the sewing machine with cotton thread, which is preferable when stitching natural fibres together. It is stronger than polyester and will better tolerate the heat of the iron. Test the stitch using a sample sandwich of the fabrics you are about to sew and check the stitch tension; the seam should not be tight or pucker, but neither should it be loose – if you pull the seam apart to mimic the strain it will get in use, a ladder should not be evident.

Always use an appropriate stitch length. Will what you are stitching be under any strain? In the case of the bodice, yes, it will, so I would recommend a medium-sized stitch at about 10 stitches per 2.5cm. As a general rule choose the largest stitch suitable for the purpose: you will find it much easier to unpick in the event of a mistake.

Stitch these five pinned sections. Backstitch inside the boundaries of the finished bodice, not where you start and finish sewing at the raw edge. Stitch all the panels one after another and then clip them apart, thus saving thread and adding speed.

Accurately pin together the bodice sections starting at the waist to the high hip line, and then to the top edge. They should fit exactly.

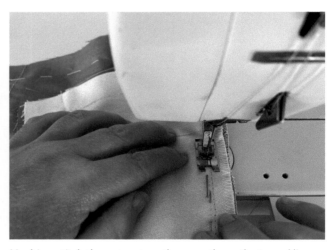

Machine-stitch the seams together exactly on the traced lines.

Pressing

Pressing is a vital process and makes a huge difference in achieving a professional finish. Do a test first to see if your fabric marks under the iron. If it does, you will need to use a pressing cloth.

STEP 1: Use a steam iron to first press the stitch line flat, using the toe of the iron at points like the bust seam where curves are present. You will have gone to a lot of trouble to add shape to your garment. It is about to become a three-dimensional shape which will clothe the curves of the body, so respect this and don't flatten out any of the shaping.

STEP 2: Use a sleeve board and tailor's ham if you have one to echo the areas on the body over which the panels will sit. Pressing from the wrong side, push the seam allowances away from you. Work from the high hip line to the waist and then from the top edge to the waist, pressing the allowances together and away from you. Then turn the section around and reverse the process.

STEP 3: Finally, press the seam open, first using the toe of the iron, and then the plate. You are aiming to get a crisp finish, with the panel pieces accurately pressed out to their fullest extent.

STEP 4: It may be possible to finish pressing your seam from the right side, but make sure the fabric does not become shiny and the overlocking does not leave a mark. A pressing cloth can help prevent damage to the top fabric.

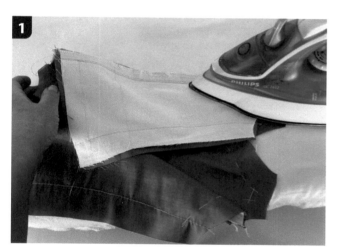

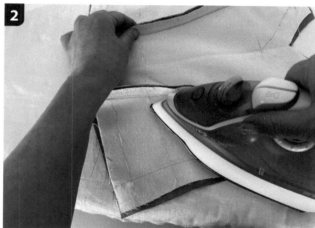

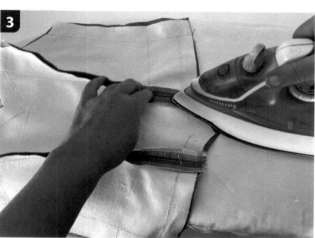

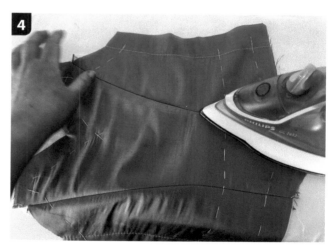

Joining the remaining sections

If making the larger sizes, join the remaining CF and SF/SSF panels together, pinning in the opposite direction, so that when machined, the bodice does not twist. Press these seams carefully using the ham. Finally, join the side seams in the same direction but using a large stitch as these seams will need to come apart after the fitting. Leave these remaining seam allowances unfinished.

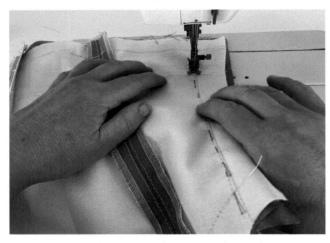

Sew the seam in the opposite direction to those adjacent.

Shoulder straps

Use a safety pin to attach the elastic shoulder straps with a 2.5cm seam allowance at the front at the junction with the neckline, as described in Chapter 2. It looks neater and less distracting in the fitting if the seam allowance is on the inside. Check the back elastic strap position from the first fitting and pin a 7.5cm extension into place on the top line on the outside of the bodice, so that any adjustments needed can be done from the back.

The bodice is now ready for a second fitting. The following options are suggestions which vary from the examples, but you may like to incorporate them into your design at this stage.

Piping as decoration

Piping the seam lines can look very effective and help to accentuate a style line, but keep to seams like the SF/SSF which are unlikely to alter. Piping can be made either with a matching or contrast fabric. This design decision should be made before the bodice is overlocked and assembled. Work out how much piping you need. Then cut the bias strips 3.2cm wide and the length required for each seam. Avoid joining these sections if at all possible. Follow the Step 1 instructions in Chapter 5 to create the piping then stitch onto the bodice and neaten the raw edges of both piping and bodice seam allowance at the same time.

Sleeves

The sleeves we will deal with here are delicate, diaphanous lengths of soft net. These can either be on an armband, or take the form of a draped strip which contains an elasticated channel that joins to the shoulder straps at the junction of the bodice. Make a prototype to check the effect you want, and fit at the second fitting to give you an idea of the finished costume. Check the length and also the density of the net – you may want to add more, or change its depth.

An armband sleeve

The length of the strip you need to make the armband will be dependent on the density of your net. Start by taking the upper arm measurement and multiplying by three. The depth of the frill will again depend on the effect you want, but I would suggest 18cm for an adult and 10cm for a child. This is the deepest it should be; narrow the depth where it meets at the underarm to about 10cm and 6cm respectively. Draft a pattern using these dimensions – keep the upper edge straight, and narrow the lower edge that will sit under the arm as it approaches the underarm point. Two layers of net per sleeve can look pretty: it's up to you.

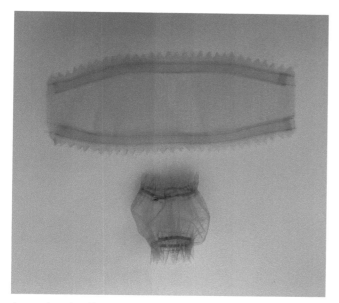

An armband cuff.

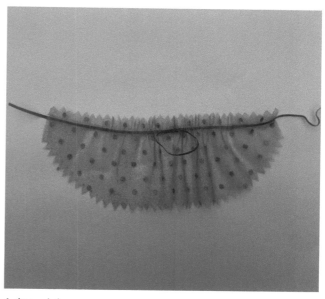

A draped sleeve.

Scallop or point the top and bottom edges of the net using the small template you used to edge the tutu skirt. Make a channel from a strip of net, wide enough to carry your elastic plus 1cm to allow for seam allowances – 0.5mm on each side. Pin on 2.5cm down from the upper edge to give a heading. Finish each end of the channel 2.5cm before the seamline by folding under the ends to add strength. Stitch onto the sleeve 0.5mm from each side of the cut edge of the channel. If you have decided to use a double layer of net, pin them together and treat them as one; they can always be tweaked apart later with a puff of steam from the iron. Stitch the two narrow ends of the sleeve together with an overlaid seam. Insert 5mm flesh-coloured elastic through the channel using a safety pin; this should be the length of the dancer's arm plus 2.5cm. You will need to fit this on the dancer – make sure the elastic is tight enough to stay up but not so tight it is uncomfortable. Secure with a small safety pin ready for the second fitting.

An armband cuff can be made in a similar way. Make a second channel at the bottom of a straight strip of double net, and thread elastic through as before.

A draped sleeve

To make a drape that starts at the shoulder strap on the front, goes around the arm and links at the back shoulder strap, take the length from shoulder strap to shoulder strap around the outside of the arm – about 30cm for a child and 50cm for an adult. To draft a pattern, multiply this measurement by anywhere between 0.25 and 2 depending on the effect required to give the length of the net strip needed. Doubling the length will give an appreciable frill; multiplying by 0.25 will give a gentler effect but still allow for easy movement. The strip should be at its deepest at the outside of the arm, about 18cm for an adult and 10cm for a child, and should narrow to about 7cm for an adult and 4cm for a child at the junction with the bodice.

Create a paper pattern and then pin this onto the net. Cut two layers of net per sleeve. These could be the same net used for the tutu plate or you may have found a fancy net or lace to use as the top layer.

Scallop or point each net edge with the smallest template used on the tutu. Also cut a channel the length of the sleeve and 2.5cm wide. Pin this 2.5cm down from the top edge to create a heading and machine-stitch 0.5mm from each of the channel edges. Insert a length of 5mm elastic through the channel: allow 60cm for an adult and 40cm for a child. You will need to double-check the length of this at the fitting. A separate band of elastic (approximately 18cm long for an adult, 14cm for a teenager and 10cm for a child) will sit around the upper arm and ensure the drape will return to its correct position after the arm has been raised and prevent it getting caught on the shoulder. Distribute the sleeve gathers along the elastic and then stitch the armband loop about halfway along the sleeve length on the inside. Use a safety pin to join the elastics to the junction of the front shoulder strap from the inside with a 2.5cm seam allowance. At the back, use a safety pin to join the back shoulder strap on the outside with a 7.5cm seam allowance so it can be easily altered in the second fitting.

CHAPTER 5

The Second Fitting and Finishing the Bodice

The costume is starting to take shape by this stage, and you are over halfway to completing it. The important second fitting is a chance to check the fit of the basic costume before completion. Any fitting issues will be easy to spot and correcting at this stage will be far simpler than when it is finished.

The second fitting

The second fitting requires the finished tutu plate, the bodice to be assembled in the top fabric but with the top, bottom and CB lines left unfinished, and any sleeves if they are part of the costume. Along with the fitting kit taken to the first fitting, it can be useful to take the notes from the original fitting to refer to. Also take along the design and any component parts of decoration or fabrics so you, the dancer and the designer can get an idea of scale and positioning, and what it will look like on the finished costume.

Before the fitting, join the tacked waistline of the bodice to the waist of the basque where the junction of the Petersham meets the fabric of the basque using safety pins. Start at the CF, then pin the CBs. You should find the bodice waistline is slightly bigger than the tutu waistband. Then pin the side seams, and then between the quarters. Finally, remove the two CB pins so the basque and tutu can be hooked up in the fitting.

At the fitting the dancer should be wearing only what they will wear under the tutu in performance, which is generally knickers and tights; it is difficult to get an accurate fit over a leotard or leggings. Get the dancer to step into the tutu, and hook it up at the waistband and high hip line. She can then post her arms through the elastic straps. Ideally, there will be a floor length mirror to hand – this is useful as the dancer will know what suits her and you can get an idea of what the costume will look like at a distance.

Before pinning the bodice together, you need to check the fit of the tutu base:

- Does the waistband fit? Dancers vary as to how tight they like the waistband. This can be readjusted at the end of the fitting, once they have become accustomed to the costume.
- Does the basque fit? It should sit snuggly on the waist. Below this, the drill should sit flat against the body all the way around to the high hip line. This is crucial to the fit of the finished costume, so adjust if necessary. It is possible to add further safety pins to use as bars, so you can hook the tutu closed again.
- Ask if the knicker leg elastics feel tight enough.

Now fit the bodice – this can alter slightly once it is made up in the top fabric. It should meet at the centre back line, so adjust if necessary.

- Are the shoulder straps tight enough? It should be obvious at this point if they need adjusting either in length or in position on the bodice.
- Does the bodice fit smoothly around the body? Around the chest? It is easier to fit with ordinary steel pins and pinch in any excess fabric. It is useful to have a mirror in the fitting room is so that you can look at the costume from a distance, which makes it easier to spot where it needs adjusting. It is easiest to modify the size at the side seams, but it may be necessary to adjust the SF/SSF line too.

- When the dancer does a back bend, is the top tack line high enough? If not, mark a new line with safety pins.
- Look at the proportions in the mirror – is the top line flattering? Does it sit under the shoulder blade at the back? Re-mark using safety pins if the line needs to be different from the tacked line.

If during the fitting you know it doesn't fit but are unsure what needs to be altered, don't panic! Most costume-makers experience this feeling. The important thing is just to make the bodice fit onto the dancer's body while they are with you and then refine the alterations when you get back to the studio and can think through the issues.

Fit the bodice by pinning up the CB, adjusting the marked line if necessary.

Check that the bodice fits smoothly around the body. Adjust the shoulder elastics if necessary.

Check the bodice back sits beneath the shoulder blade. Check the tutu is sitting horizontally and is the desired shape.

Fitting the sleeves

Armband sleeves

If you are fitting the style of sleeve which sits at the top of the arm with an elastic armband, check the elastic is tight enough – the balance between it being tight enough to stay in place but not so tight that it is uncomfortable needs to be found. If at the second fitting it does not stay in place, it is possible to add a 'gummy' elastic. This type of rubber finish is a little like that used on hold-up stockings and helps the sleeves or shoulder straps to stay in place during the performance. Finally, check the depth of the sleeves and quantity of fabric used – are you satisfied with the proportions of these?

Draped sleeves

It is useful to have pinned draped sleeves into place before the fitting, so the length of the elastic and its positioning can now be checked. Check the proportions of everything in the mirror – are you happy with their depth and balance?

Check the armband is the correct length and positioned correctly on the sleeve band.

Armband sleeves.

Draped sleeves.

The additional loop of elastic which sits around the top of the arm will ensure the sleeve will return to its correct position after the arm is raised and then lowered, and it will not get stuck on the shoulder.

Final checks

Take an overall view of the basic costume:

- Does it look well proportioned?
- Is the tutu lying horizontally? Occasionally you will find it tips slightly, most likely up at the back like a 'duck's tail'. This can happen if the dancer has a pronounced bottom. If the dancer is 'sway' waisted, the opposite can happen.
- Is the shape of the tutu plate or drop what you were expecting? Remember the hoop hasn't been finished off yet, and the masking tape can be adjusted in the fitting if you feel it needs it; push more into the channel if it you want it to be flatter, or remove some if the tutu needs a deeper drop.

Now work on the decoration and its proportion. Are there any ideas you want to try out?

Take a final look at the costume in the mirror from a distance, and if you are happy with it, take photographs, especially of any alterations or things you may need to be reminded of later. Mark the CB of the bodice with pencil on the inside if it differs from the hand-tacked line and remove those safety pins so the dancer can get out of the costume.

It is important to take notes as you go along, especially if you are doing more than one fitting at a time. The photographs will help with this. I often take a picture of the name label so I know all the images before this picture refer to that dancer's costume.

Check the proportions from a distance. Is the tutu the desired shape? Do any sleeves balance the design and allow for full movement?

Try out any design ideas while the designer or client is there.

This is the time to see how the embellishment will read from a distance. Try out your ideas to see what works and what could be improved.

Trouble-shooting

Duck's tail

If the tutu rises up at the back, it creates a shape that is sometimes described in the profession as a 'duck's tail'. This is due to the basque not sitting in the correct place; it is generally because the basque is too small on the high hip. Hopefully, this will have been picked up at the second fitting. To rectify this, release the hook at the high hip, ensure the waistband is located on the natural waist, and measure the extra required at the high hip to make it sit level. If this is less than 2.5cm, simply shift the bar of the hook fastening over. If the difference is greater than this, or you are making for a young dancer who has grown, you should keep the CB symmetrical and let out the basque at the sides, which will mean restitching the knicker on. The basque has been constructed to make this a straightforward process and the knicker was also drafted with excess to allow for adjustments of this nature. This may seem a fiddly job, but it is well worth the effort.

Fluting

This occurs when the high hip is too big and the excess net appears to make furrows at the CB. Unpick the knicker from the basque, make any adjustments necessary to the basque to make it fit and sit nicely on the dancer. Try not to gather the knicker back onto the basque; instead, make a dart in the knicker to make it sit better, if possible. A top skirt can exacerbate the fluting problem if the high hip measurement on the top skirt is greater than that of the knicker and basque. One solution would be to make a tuck in the CB of the top skirt to reduce the fabric quantity and help to give the appearance of a flatter area to the tutu.

Completing the tutu and finishing the hoop

Make any corrections to the tutu. Although it is possible to let the CB in and out with additional bars, if it is a bespoke tutu, any alterations should be done on the side seams so the tutu remains symmetrical and balanced. This may require removing the knicker, adjusting the basque side seams equally and then reattaching the tutu.

Once the final length of the hoop has been decided, it can be finished off properly. If it is plastic or plastic-coated hoop, bind it with zinc oxide tape, matching-coloured sticky tape, electrician's tape or masking tape. If you are using a steel hoop with a cotton cover, stitch in place by hand using a double cotton thread, and then bind the sharp cut edges with tape to prevent injury. It is good practice to cover the adhesive tape with a fabric binding as the tape can become sticky over time. Simply wrap a length of cotton tape or bias binding around the join and stitch into place with a double cotton thread. When the hoop has been joined, reshuffle the nets on the hoop layer around the join to spread the gathers evenly.

The knicker elastics need a 2.5cm overlap, so remove any excess elastic and hand-stitch into place securely with a double cotton thread. Tuck the junction into the bias binding so it looks neat.

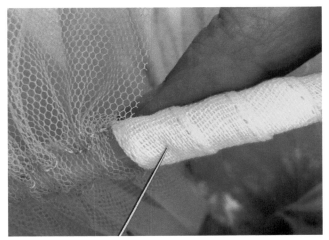

Once the correct length of the hoop has been established, it can be closed by binding with zinc oxide tape, and then wrapping in cotton tape. Hold in place with a few stitches.

Finishing the bodice

Marking the alterations

Look at any modifications made in the fitting. Mark any alterations on the wrong side of the bodice with the vanishing pen and remove the safety pins. If the costume includes sleeves, mark the pitch points on the bodice and on the sleeve where the seams of the bodice hit, as this will help with positioning them accurately. Then take the bodice pattern or original calico toile and begin to transfer the modifications, making sure to adjust any asymmetry – sometimes in a fitting it is easy to accidently pin out more on one side than the other. As long as this was accidental, take an average of the two measurements and use that.

The CB should remain on the straight grain, so if the alteration is not parallel with it, you will need to adjust the CB/SB or side seam to accommodate the alteration.

Undo the side seams; as these were sewn with a large stitch, they should come apart easily. Unpick any seams you need to alter on the CF/SFs or SB/CB seams and transfer all the altered markings from the pattern to the bodice with a pencil. Hand-tack the CB if it has changed. Then leaving the side seams open until they have been piped, restitch the rest of the bodice with a small to medium stitch. You should be left with a single front section and two back sections.

Prepare the CB closure

STEP 1: Place the two CB sections in front of you with the wrong sides facing up. The one on the left-hand side will finish on the CB line – this is the side which will be cut away, hold the boning, and have the hooks stitched onto it. The right-hand side will have the extension which holds the bars.

On the left side use a pencil to mark a 3.5cm seam allowance line on the wrong side. On the right side you will need a 5cm extension, which matches the extension you have on the basque. Mark two pencil lines in the seam allowance at 5cm and 10cm from the CB line.

Machine-stitch all these pencil lines and the CBs with a medium-sized stitch, and then overlock, cutting away the excess so the overlocking stitch sits outside the stitched line. This will mean when you later come to fold back the side which will hold the bars, you will be able to stitch neatly from the right side, confident that the return is being trapped.

STEP 2: To neaten the side seams, mark 3cm from the finished side seam line on the wrong side on all four side seam pieces (2 × SF or SSF sections and 2 × SB sections). Machine-stitch down these pencil lines to join the top fabric to the backing fabric. At the junction of the waistline and seam allowance, stitch a zigzagged box, a little like the three sides of a buttonhole which was used on the knicker opening. Clip into this about 1cm, and then overlock the side seam on the stitched line, ensuring you pull the clipped waistline apart as you stitch over it; the overlocking stitch has the ability to stretch quite a lot as you stitch over the gap, which will enable you to clip into the waist later in order to press it flat.

STEP 3: Always clip as little as necessary to enable you to let out the costume at a later date. You may need to clip slightly further into the seam allowance after you have stitched the side seam in order to press it flat, but this is a decision that can be made later.

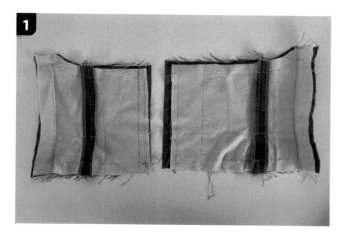

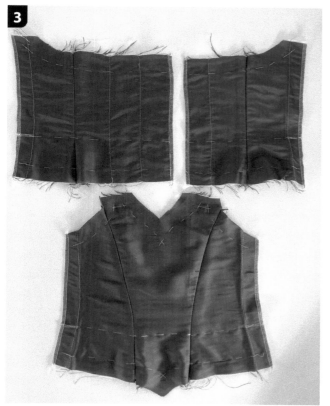

Make the piping

STEP 1: Take the pre-shrunk 00 piping cord, and the bias strips you cut earlier from the top fabric; have the wrong side facing up and using a zipper foot, fold a third of the width of the strip over the piping cord. Sew close to the cord using a long stitch; you will tighten the fit of the fabric around the cord with a second row of stitching when you come to attach it to the bodice. Don't worry about backstitching as you will need to unpick the end in order to fold in the raw edge. Repeat this process with all the separate cut strips.

STEP 2: Neaten the remaining raw edge by folding it in to meet the one encasing the piping cord and edge-stitch into place. I find this process easiest with an all-purpose machine presser foot, but you may need to alter the needle position in order to get a neat result. Alternatively, you can use a zipper foot or buttonhole foot if you find this easier.

By this point you should be able to get an idea of the exact length of piping sections you will need. The top piped edge will require the longest piece, especially if there is no CF seam, so ensure to set aside enough piping as this edge will be attached last. Only join the bias strips if you are short of fabric, as the seams can be bulky.

Piping the bodice

The piping gets applied in three sections to the high hip line to make it easier to alter in the future. The top line is piped in one or two sections depending on whether there is a CF seam, and the fact that the top edge contains an acute angle at the side seam which if altered is easier to re-pipe in one. Begin by piping the high hip sections in three separate pieces; these sections each finish on the side seam.

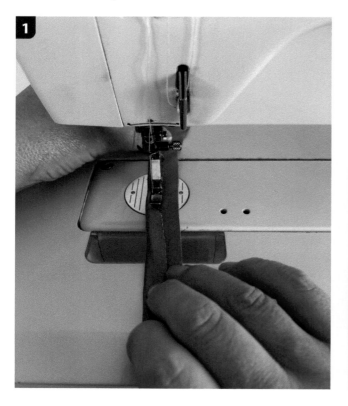

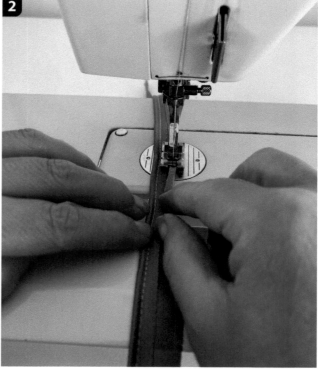

STEP 1: Pin back the seam allowances on the bodice, so they don't get flipped out of place as you stitch over them from the right side. Fold the right-hand side back onto the CB line, and fold the left-hand side back onto the 5cm extension line, matching the finished closure. The piping on the high hip line needs to start on the CB line on the right-hand side, and extend 5cm beyond the CB line on the left-hand side. This means if you ever need to alter the position of the bars, there will be a neat, piped edge visible on the extension. Mark these points with cross pins, to remind you where to start and stop.

Use an all-purpose presser foot, or you could use a buttonhole foot as the cord will sit neatly into a groove on the underside, giving you control and accuracy. Test the stitch on some spare fabric and adjust the needle position if necessary to achieve a neat, tight piping. Sometimes the sewing machine may falter when you start stitching; this is common when there are too many different levels for it to cope with. Lay the piping in position, but begin by hand-cranking the needle into position 1cm beyond the start line. You should then be able to start with a backstitch and then stitch smoothly forward as normal.

STEP 2: I can apply the piping without pinning it on first, by stretching out the bodice and gently placing the piping on top. Try this approach, as it is not as difficult as it sounds and it cuts out the pinning process. The most important thing is to ensure the bodice section does not tighten up, so pull the bodice out flat and ensure the piping is not stretched but gently put into place.

When you are happy with the technique, work out which end of the cord you need to finish – remember when you stitch it on, the cord will lean towards the bodice and the neatened, stitched edge towards the raw edge of the bodice. Begin by unpicking two or three stitches on the cord stitch line, open out the bias strip and cut the end neatly at 90 degrees before folding in a 5mm raw edge to neaten it. You will be left with a small piece of visible piping cord.

Start by piping the high hip line from the CB to the side seam, aiming to stitch the piping straight on top of the stitching line marking the finished edge of the high hip. Begin with a backstitch to secure it and stop stitching

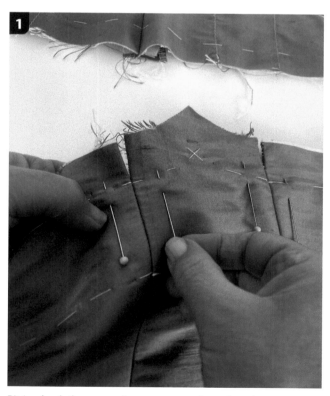

Pining back the seam allowances guards against them getting trapped out of place as you stitch on the piping.

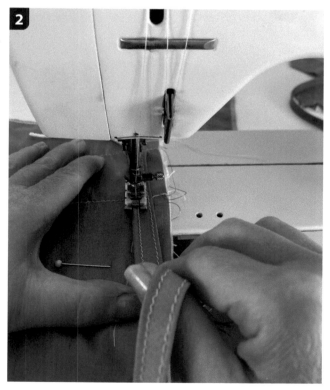

An all-purpose foot or buttonhole foot work well for stitching on the piping. Test your skills on some spare fabric to ensure the line is accurate and the piping doesn't tighten up before embarking on the bodice.

about 5cm before the end. Leave the needle in the fabric and prepare the folded end before stitching to the end of the side seam allowance and securing. Repeat on the back section with the extension, beginning at the cross pins – the edge which will eventually get folded back.

STEP 3: Then pipe the front section from side seam allowance to side seam allowance. If this section has a CF point, leave the needle in the down position when you reach the CF seam, and then turn the bodice and piping – you may need to squash down the cord with some scissors to avoid stitching a pleat into the bias, or you may later need to cut a couple of stitches when you trim the allowances back in order for it to sit flat.

STEP 4: Remove the hand-tacking on the piped edge. If the bodice is likely to be altered for other dancers, it is good practice to leave the 2.5cm seam allowance in place and not trim it away. This gives the opportunity to alter it for dancers with a longer body. Otherwise, trim back the seam allowances with sharp scissors. The seams were backstitched within the boundary of the bodice panel so they will not come apart. Then turn back the top fabric and drill to a width that will not show once the piping has been pressed back, and trim the drill to half that width. Continue trimming the CB sections beyond where the piping stops as these will be turned back when the CB is finished.

STEP 5: Press the piping into place from the wrong side. Pin the side seams together in preparation for finishing the top edge. Match the waistlines first, and then the rest of the seam can be pinned together.

STEP 6: Hand-sew the piping to the high hip line with a few stab stitches to ensure the seam does not shift when stitching the side seam.

STEP 7: Machine-stitch the side seam, backstitching for strength within the boundaries of the bodice.

STEP 8: Press the seams flat and then open, clipping further into the buttonhole if necessary.

STEP 9: By piping the top edge in two sections, with the break at the CF (if you have the design with a seam on the CF), you will have the ability to tighten the piping cord over the bust after the final fitting. As the angle

at the top edge side seam will be quite acute, any alteration will make a 'step', so for this reason I put a pleat discreetly in the SB section of the piping which can be unpicked and re-piped in the event of an alteration.

Begin by pinning back the seam allowances as before, and adding pins to the point where the piping stops on the CB sections, which will be at the same point as the lower edge. Also use pins to mark the section between the area on the SB panel where there are no turnings, as this is where the pleat will sit in the event of letting the bodice out in the future, and it is easy to forget if you do not mark it. Visually check the appearance of the top tacked line. There can sometimes be a small discrepancy between the tacks. Even them up if necessary and make sure the bodice is symmetrical.

Beginning at the CB hook side, neaten the edge as before and stitch on the piping. Just before you reach the seam allowance of the SB and SF/SSF side seam, backstitch, lift the foot and the needle, put in a 2.5cm fold of the piping to create a pleat, and stitch again, ensuring you stitch over the previous stitching line so this will be almost invisible on the right side.

Stop before you get to the CF seam and prepare the end; you will need to have an extra length of piping cord of about 5cm in the event that you need to tighten the line over the bust to make it fit better and feel more secure. Cut the piping here, and then make the neatened top fabric edge back at the point the top line meets the CF seam.

Repeat on the second side of the bodice, with the extra piping cord length on the CF, the pleat on the SB section and finish with the extra 5cm over the CB line. Trim back and press as before. It is possible to have a join at the CF if there is no seam there, or you may decide to pipe the entire top edge in one piece.

To complete the piped edges, slip-stitch back all the piped edges by hand using a double thread. Be careful to only catch the drill backing; if you come through to the right side of the fabric the stitches will show and look unsightly. The side seam allowances will need to be stab-stitched back on the high hip line in the ditch of the piping cord.

Finishing the centre back closure

Starting with the CB hook side, get rid of any bulk on the fold by trimming a 'V' into the seam allowance to enable it to be folded back neatly.

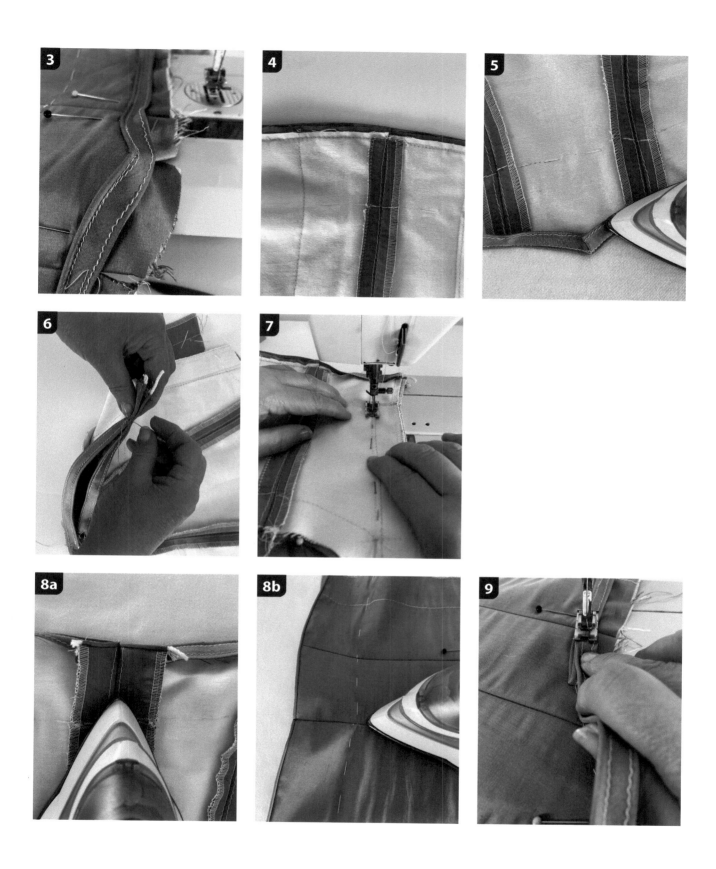

Press along the pre-stitched CB line, then edge-stitch the CB from the right side, which will provide a crisp edge. Cut a spiral steel bone using pliers or wire cutters; use 7mm-wide boning that is 1.5cm shorter than the length of the CB. Finish the ends with bone caps and insert the bone into the bodice – the ends should be inserted into the fold of the drill so they are secured by the piping and won't fall out. Then stitch a neat, tight channel to encase the boning using a zipper foot.

As with the tutu plate, your finished costume will look professional if you machine-stitch a name label onto the CB extension before stitching back the bar side.

Press back the extension side on the 5cm line; the overlocked edge should extend slightly beyond the CB line when folded back to enable you to pin and stitch from the right side. Machine-stitch exactly on top of the existing CB line and then stitch a second 'tramline' about 2mm into the extension allowance. Hand slip-stitch back the top and bottom edges within the extension to neaten them off. Neatly trim off any visible piping cord.

Stab-stitch the side seam allowances at the lower edge so they lie flat.

Hooks and bars

STEP 1: Each of the size 3 dress hooks and bars are

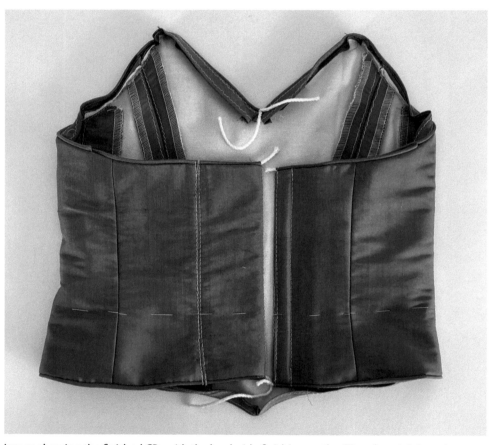

Image showing the finished CBs with the hook side finishing on the CB and containing a bone and the left side showing the extension and double row of stitching which will hold the bars.

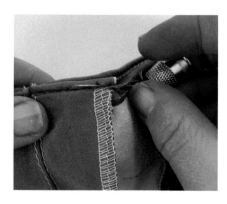

Stab-stitch the side seam allowances at the lower edge so they lie flat.

stitched on separately. Generally, hook and bar tape is not used, particularly as costumes are widely shared by dancers, so many costumes have several rows of bars to accommodate fluctuations in size or changes in casting. Start by marking the position of the hooks with a small pencil dot. The space a bar takes up is wider than that of a hook, so the hooks positioned at the top and bottom edges should be set in slightly from the piped edge. It is important there is a hook on the waist, so mark this first; followed by the top and bottom hooks. The remaining hooks should be evenly spread between 3–4cm apart.

Use a cotton four-thread to stitch on the hooks. Set the head of the hook back from the edge slightly – remember the bodice will be under some strain when it is done up and the head of the hook shouldn't show. Hide the knot within the inside of the turn-back and make three stitches through each loop, coming neatly through to the right side with a prick stitch, then travel invisibly through the fabric and place two stitches at the 'neck' of the hook, again coming all the way through to

the right side, exactly onto the stitch line used to trap the bone. Finally, stitch the head of the hook firmly down, sewing onto the edge-stitched machine line and finish off with three small stitches. When all of the hooks have been stitched on, the CB return can be slip-stitched into place.

STEP 2: Now mark the position of the bars by laying the CBs on top of each other and marking pencil dots within the tramline to line up with the hooks.

STEP 3: The bars are made from a length of brass or nickel, and the breaks in the wire should be set towards the hook, so that when it is done up and under tension, the thread is unlikely to find this break and come off. Use a four-thread to make three stitches in each of the loops and then fasten off neatly. Avoid making a large knot on the inside which could irritate the dancer's skin.

Shoulder straps

STEP 1: To stitch on the shoulder straps, take a four-thread in the same colour as the bodice. Place the elastic on the inside of the bodice at the junction marked at the fitting, and with a 2.5cm extension at the front. Stab-stitch the elastic through the ditch in the piping with three 1.5cm long stitches on top of each other. Fasten off and then use herringbone stitch to attach the remaining shoulder strap onto the inside of the bodice.

STEP 2: Then repeat the process for attaching the strap at the back. The 7.5cm excess can be used in future alterations.

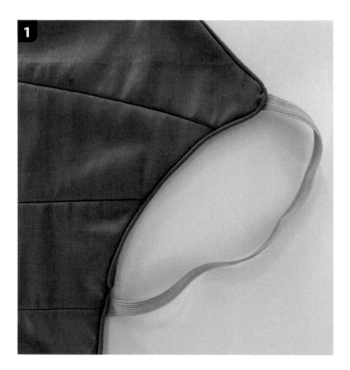

Sleeves

Add these after the shoulder straps and, in the same way as the shoulder strap, leave a 2.5cm piece of elastic at the front and around 7.5cm at the back. Stab-stitch the elastic to the bodice over the shoulder straps and use herringbone stitch to sew down the elastic extension to the inside of the bodice. You will also need to link the lower edges of each net sleeve with a small stitch to stop them slipping away from the bodice. Attach a loop of elastic which will sit around the arm and ensure the drape will return to its original position after the arm has been raised.

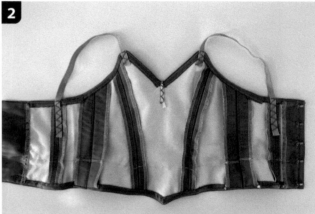

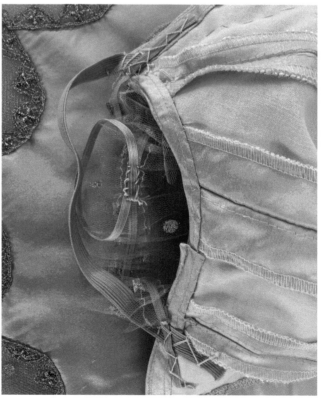

Attaching draped sleeves.

A CF infill for a low neckline

STEP 1: At the first fitting, the depth of the CF neckline will have been established. If this is particularly low, you will need to create an infill from a flesh-coloured fabric like illusion fabric, souffle or minx net in order to help the bodice to maintain its structure. Create the pattern from the toile; it should be the exact shape of the area of bodice that was removed when the bodice was piped. The CF of the infill should be placed on a fold when you cut it whether or not this is the case with the bodice. The infill fabric has a one-way stretch, is strong and comes in a flesh tone, or it can be dyed to match. Cut a double layer of fabric with the stretch going up and down the body, as it should not stretch widthways and distort the bodice. Add a 1cm seam allowance at the top edge, and 2.5cm on the other two sides. These fabrics do not fray, so the edges will remain unfinished inside the bodice. Stitch the two layers of fabric together along the top edge, trim back to 5mm and clip if there is a curve. Stitch back the turnings on one side only – this will be the wrong side so the stitching is less visible on the right side of the costume. Press the fabric, with the turnings trapped on the inside, and then machine thread-mark the remaining lines.

STEP 2: Hand-tack the balance mark on the bodice where the infill meets the CF panel and then pin through the ditch in the piping into the machine thread-mark line. It should not look wrinkled, so adjust it if necessary.

STEP 3: Machine-stitch into place, and then hand-stitch the raw edges of the infill to the reverse side of the bodice with a double-thread herringbone stitch to stop them flipping over.

Boning the bodice

Sometimes for an adult costume I bone the CF panel with steel spiral boning to keep it flat, taut and in shape. It may also be necessary to bone the SF seams for a dancer with a large bust. Keep bones away from the side seam as they bulge when the dancer bends. Any boning should be added at the very end of the bodice construction so they can be easily removed. Cut the 7mm boning to size, about 1.5cm shorter than the seam. Create a casing by edge-stitching cotton 10mm India tape to make a channel wide enough to contain the boning. Cut this channel 3cm longer than the boning, insert the boning and turn over 1.5cm of the India tape at each end before pinning to the seam allowance, centring it on the seam. In order to be effective, it needs to be stitched into the seam while the bodice is pulled out to its furthest extent. Use a double cotton thread and hand-stitch using a herringbone stitch. Costumes for children or young adults should not need boning other than the CB.

Give the bodice a final press to make it look as good as possible. The bodice and tutu plate are now ready to be embellished before assembling the costume.

Boning the bodice.

CHAPTER 6

Decoration

The decoration on the costume should be made separately from the costume and stitched onto a net base before application to the tutu plate and bodice. This is mostly dictated by the aftercare of the tutu, as decoration can be removed, the tutu washed and, if necessary, the bodice can be dry-cleaned before reassembly. It also will enable you to change the design of your costume easily by replacing the decoration, giving it an entirely different look.

Creating the decoration bases

The patterns can be made with any spare net you have to hand, or if making a set of costumes I favour using strong, transparent plastic which can be purchased from a builder's merchant. Plastic can be easily marked with felt-tip pens which will show through the net bases, enabling a production line to create matching top skirts.

Preparing the tutu plate decoration base

Take a spare piece of net or piece of plastic sheet larger than the tutu plate and use a felt-tip pen and metre rule to mark a line across the centre. This will be the CF/CB line. Follow this with another line that bisects at 90 degrees to the first, creating a cross; this will be matched to the side seams.

STEP 1: Do up the closures on the CB of the tutu and tuck the basque down out of the way. The body is oval in shape, so to echo this, pin a piece of tape from the CF high hip line to the CB high hip line. This should be about 20cm for an adult, 17.5cm for a teenager and 15cm for a child. Now place the pattern on top of the tutu plate: the cross should hover over the centre of the tutu. Match the CF and CB lines first, and then locate and match the side seams.

STEP 2: Pin around the high hip line, distorting the pattern as little as possible, and then pin the pattern flat onto the tutu towards its outside edge.

STEP 3: Next, use a vanishing pen to mark the position of the high hip line and that of the CB opening, slightly beyond the opening on the tutu plate to ensure the decorative top skirt will not be under any strain when the dancer is putting the costume on. Then mark the outside edge of the tutu plate. Using a vanishing pen means any accidental markings onto the tutu will vanish in time. Then remove the pins and pattern from the tutu, and before the pen marks vanish, fold the pattern in half, first along the side seam line and then the CF/CB line, looking for any inconsistencies between the two sides.

STEP 4: Use a permanent marker to correct any irregularities by marking between the two lines; or if they are identical, well done! You can now permanently mark the high hip line and the outside edge, which is generally where the top skirt ends. If you decide to make the top skirt a different length, either longer or shorter, mark a second line parallel to the outside edge.

STEP 5: After creating the pattern, the net base onto which the decoration is placed can be made. For the plate, use the same net used for the tutu so it is unnoticeable in the final costume, unless there is a design decision to use a contrast colour. Take a piece of net slightly larger than the pattern and machine-stitch a cross through the centre in a colour which will be inconspicuous in the finished tutu.

STEP 6: Lay the net back on the flat pattern and mark the high hip line, CF, SSs and position of the CB opening. Machine thread-mark these lines.

STEP 7: Fold the base into quarters and mark the scalloped or pointed edge, generally using the same large template as used for the tutu. This time you are adding the finish to a curve rather than a straight, so adjust the template as you move around the arc. Cut the decorative edge and then open out the net to a single layer.

STEP 8: Finally, stitch in the CB opening, first with a straight stitch about 3mm from the CB line, making an arrowhead at the base of the opening and turning to stitch back up to the high hip line. Finish this edge by cutting down between the lines, folding on the stitch line and stitch down using a small zigzag stitch for strength.

Preparing the bodice decoration base

Create the bodice pattern in a similar way, by using a piece of spare net or plastic sheet, which is longer and wider than the bodice section, and draw the CF line and adjacent waistline. Now pin it in place on the finished bodice and draw on the bodice top line, high hip line and SF seams with the vanishing marker pen. Remove the pattern from the bodice and fold in half along the CF line. Note any irregularities between the two sides, and use a permanent marker to mark the corrected symmetrical lines.

Take a rectangular piece of net that matches the bodice colour and is slightly larger than the bodice decoration panel. Machine thread-mark the CF line and waistline. Much of this net will be trimmed away when you come to attach it to the bodice, but it is useful to have these lines to locate it accurately. The net base is now ready to receive the decoration.

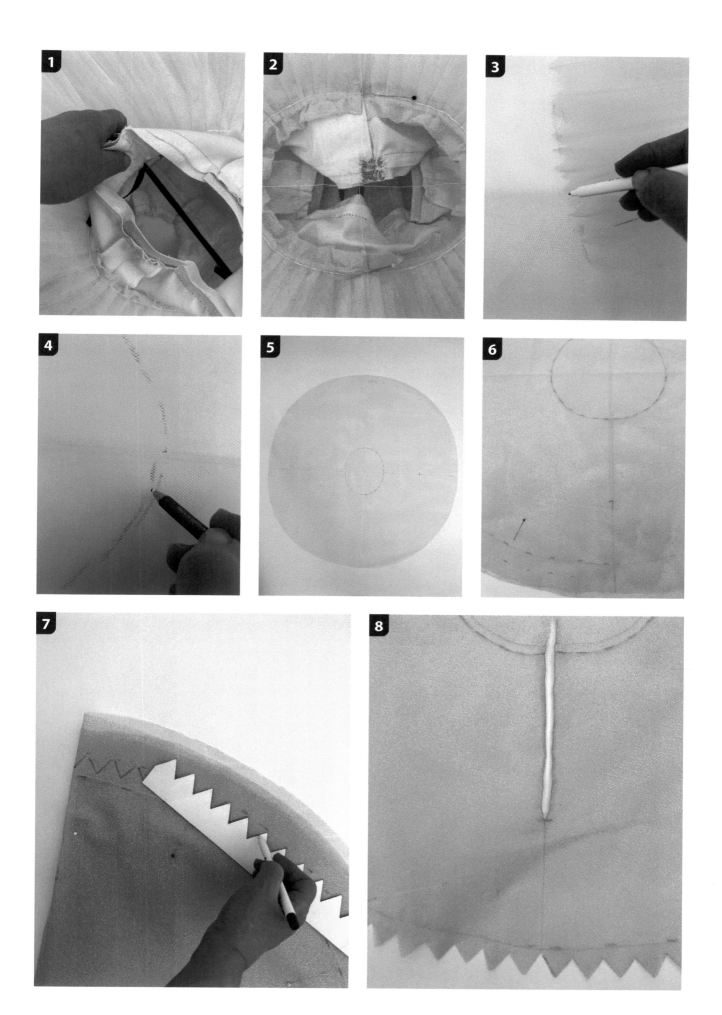

Devising the decoration

You can either copy the example decoration or create your own design.

Designing your own decoration

If you decide to create your own decoration, refer back to the ideas that you gathered during the design stage and observations from the second fitting.

Assemble the fabrics and decorations you wish to use; this could be a selection of fabrics, braids, laces, motifs, hotfix stones, decorative nets, flowers, feathers, bows and so on.

Be aware of the distance from which your costume will be seen; although small details will not show, texture and contrasts will read from the stage. Half-close your eyes or check your work in a mirror to give an illusion of distance. Swarovski or similar hotfix stones are especially good value and come alive under lighting. They come in many sizes and colours.

Lightly pin the net bases to the tutu and bodice. It can be very helpful to pin on different arrangements of the decoration, recording each with digital pictures, before deciding what works and then spending time refining the best one.

It is often possible to cut motifs from decorative lace or braids and then reassemble them to create panels which suit the area to be decorated.

Once the basic ideas have been established, you can start to adapt them into a more refined pattern. Remove the net bases from the plate and bodice, and place back onto the original base patterns. If you want to add fabric sections like the petals on the top skirt of the white design, cut out paper shapes, refining them until you are happy with the scale and dimensions.

You can make a pattern from a thick type of transparent plastic you can find in builder's merchants. Place this over the original pattern and copy the central CF to CB and side seam cross and high hip lines, including the CB opening, using felt-tip pens before drawing the design features straight onto the plastic to ensure these features are placed symmetrically. This method is also useful if you are making a set of costumes and want to apply any glued decoration, as it will peel straight off and can be used to make sure the next top skirt is identical.

Play around with the look, then take a step back and consider the effect. Look at the proportions: are they flattering? They should enhance the dancer's shape and the character they are portraying. Generally, you want to make the waist look slim, so the decoration should grow from this narrowest area. Keep refining until you are happy with the result. If the dancer you are making for is likely to be partnered and you plan decoration around the waist, this area needs to be smooth for the partner's comfort, and it also needs to be robust enough to withstand constant handling. Small hotfix stones will be fine, but may need replacing from time to time. Avoid too much decoration around the bodice fastenings as this will get a lot of wear and is therefore unlikely to last.

Any decorative bodice panel will need to be firmly stitched to the bodice and there should be no gaps where fingers could get caught.

You may wish to add a gathered net top skirt, in which case use the pattern to gauge how much excess you wish to add – is the gather at the high hip line, extending to a flat outer edge – possibly utilising a decorative finished edge of a textile; or do you want it to sit flat on the high hip line, fluting towards the outside – in which case you may need to use sections of a circle which will need to be seamed?

The top skirt decoration should relate to the bodice, so work on them both at the same time.

Applying the decoration to the base net patterns

Start with the top skirt. Add any base fabrics first (like the ones in the pink and white designs). Begin by placing the net base onto the pattern and mark the design with the vanishing fabric marker. The fabric can then be pinned to the top side, and machine-stitched around the marked design to hold it in place. Also restitch the high hip. Trim back the excess fabric close to the stitching line and then sew using a zigzag stitch over the raw edges ensuring the unit does not 'tighten up'.

Make the opening in the CB by stitching a slim arrowhead from inside the high hip line oval to mark the opening. This should be no more than 5mm wide and should be stitched through any fabric decoration. Now cut down this slit but leave the oval at the centre of the piece to retain stability until it is finished and ready to be stitched to the tutu base. Roll under the raw edges at the CB and sew using a small zigzag stitch over the machined line leaving a strong, neat edge.

Work the bodice section in a similar way. Add any base fabric before building up the embellishment with braids and motifs.

Making bows and tabs

STEP 1: Bows or tabs benefit from an internal layer of net to add volume and lightness. This layer will also help prevent crushing. Start by pinning different arrangements onto the tutu to decide what looks best; even subtle differences in proportion can make a big difference. When you are happy, calculate the dimensions required for the bow or tab top fabric plus seam allowances. The internal net should be a similar size.

STEP 2: Stitch these two fabrics into a tube, turn through and press.

STEP 3: Stitch into the required shapes in preparation for application to the net base.

A latex contact adhesive like Copydex is useful for applying braid or trim, as you need a lot of pins and they tend to fall out of the net. Use only a tiny amount of glue and brush onto the back of the braid, wait for it to dry slightly and then apply. It is much better to 'tack' the braid on instead of using pins as it is quicker, the shapes can be easily repositioned if you are not happy with them, there is less likelihood of accidently leaving in a pin, and the panel will not be distorted, which it can be if a lot of pins are used. Check you are happy with the result before machine-stitching to the panel using a three-step zigzag stitch or similar. This will be invisible when complete, and you should make sure you comprehensively stitch down any edges which could flip up.

Take a final look at the decorative panels from a distance; does everything register as you hope? Would the effect be improved with the addition of anything else? Add any further embellishment until you are satisfied it is complete.

The decoration panels are now ready to apply to the completed tutu base and bodice, before the costume is assembled.

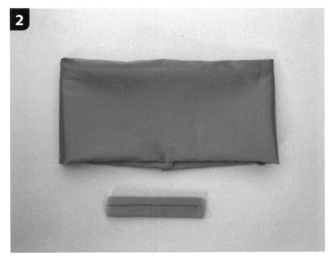

CHAPTER 7

Finishing

All the component parts – the tutu plate, bodice and decoration – will be complete by this stage and ready for assembly.

Assembling the costume

Adding the decorative panels

Begin with the tutu plate and top skirt. Double-check the measurement of the high hip line on the tutu and compare it to the equivalent line on the top skirt. It is important to ensure the top skirt does not affect the size of the costume, so the high hip line on the top skirt must be altered if it is too small. If it is larger than the tutu high hip line, it will not sit flat. If necessary, stitch a further line inside or outside the existing high hip line on the top skirt depending on whether it is too big or too small. This adjustment is subtle, but it will make a difference to the look of the finished costume.

STEP 1: The central section of the top skirt now needs removing. Stitch a further line about 10mm inside the high hip line starting and finishing at the CB opening.

STEP 2: Trim back to just outside the stitch line, clip in with small clips of about 2mm all the way around, and then neaten the raw edge using a large zig-zag stitch.

STEP 3: Stretch open the clipped edge as you stitch so it will sit well on the tutu plate and basque.

STEP 4: Pin together the tutu plate and top skirt along the high hip line. Start by connecting the CF, then the CB. Do up the basque and then evenly distribute the top skirt around the rest of the high hip line: the side seam on the basque should match the stitching line on the top skirt. Stand back and check the top skirt looks flat. If it is fighting itself or bubbling anywhere, adjust until it sits neatly while still attaching accurately to the high hip line of the tutu. Pin the outer edges of the top skirt to the tutu using glass-headed pins. Begin at the CF, then pin the CB and side seams before pinning between these points. If you are making a drop tutu, give the top skirt a little 'air' to encourage the shape.

STEP 5: Hand-stitch the high hip line using a double cotton thread. As this is the second row of hand-stitching along this line and it will not be under any strain, use a backstitch that just catches the tutu net rather than going through all the layers.

To attach the top skirt at the outer edge, invert the tutu and insert stringing stitches from the underside. The swing catches should be as invisible as possible from the top side, so use a four-thread which best matches the colour of the top skirt. Stitch about 4cm inside the outer edge with tacks about 10cm apart, catching the top couple of layers of the tutu to the top skirt and ensuring the stitch direction radiates out from the centre. As when stringing the tutu together, load up several needles so you can get into a rhythm. Tie off the catches with a 1.5cm loop. These catches will stop the top skirt bouncing up in performance.

The bodice decoration can now be pinned onto the bodice. If there is a large excess of net around the panel, trim it back, but it will be easier to position and subsequently stitch on if there is some extra net that will be removed after application. Be aware that the decoration will sit over a curved body, so ideally pin it on the stand or over a tailor's ham so it does not constrict the bodice shape. Match the waist CF on the net panel to the thread-marked line on the bodice, and then position below the waist and then up towards the neckline. Smooth out the rest of the embellishment and pin in place. Stand back and visually check it looks correct: using a mirror can be especially useful as it highlights inaccuracies. If the embellishment is symmetrical, check the top line looks the same on both sides.

Attaching the decoration can be done by sewing machine or by hand. If the preferred method is by machine, ensure the seam allowances on the inside of the bodice are not moved out of position by pinning them to keep them in place. Use a medium to large zig-zag stitch with the top thread matched to the decoration. The stitch should be large enough to be easily unpicked for cleaning or replacing the decoration.

If you would prefer to hand-stitch, use a double thread and stitch firmly but invisibly to the bodice. If the dancer is to be partnered, take extra care when attaching the CF decoration and firmly stitch down the area between the waist and the high hip line. Ensure there is nowhere that the dancer's partner could catch their fingers.

Trim back any excess base net: the use of pinking shears here helps to blend it into the bodice. Don't worry if close up the decorative base shows; it will be invisible on stage.

Match the bodice decoration CF and waistlines and pin into place.

Trim back the excess net using pinking shears.

Completing the costume

STEP 1: You are now ready to assemble the completed decorated bodice and tutu sections. Begin by pinning the CF tacked waist of the bodice to the waist of the basque at the point where the Petersham ribbon meets the drill. Then pin the bodice CBs, extending these 1mm beyond the CB basque. Smooth out the basque on the inside and pin the side seams of the bodice to the side seams of the basque by the elastics.

The ditch at the bottom of the bodice piping should exactly meet the high hip line on the tutu and hide the net heading. Pin this in place, again starting with the CF, then the CBs, and then distributing the rest smoothly around the rest of the high hip line. The bodice should be fractionally larger than the high hip on the tutu so it does not cause the tutu to constrict.

STEP 2: If the lower edge of the bodice ends with a CF point, pin around until the bodice starts to move away from the high hip line. Then pin the remaining point section just to the top one or two layers of the tutu, without going through to the basque.

STEP 3: Stitch the bodice to the tutu with a cotton four-thread which matches the bodice fabric. Working from the inside, hide the knot and start sewing about 2.5cm from the CB on the hook side; this is because you need to access the basque, and if you connect the two elements all the way to the CB, the high hip line hook and bar would be impossible to do up.

STEP 4: Backstitch the bodice all the way through to the inside of the basque. Use similar-sized stitches to those you used to attach the tutu to the knicker, but this time with the longer stitch showing on the basque and the smaller stitches lying in the ditch between the piping and bodice.

STEP 5: Continue around the rest of the high hip line until you get to the last 5cm of the CB on the bar side and finish off securely. Use can use beeswax to help strengthen the thread around the eye and stop it breaking or knotting. It is likely you will need to do this process in several sections as stitching these fabrics together is quite tough, and the thread is likely to fray, so keep the thread lengths shorter than those used for stringing.

STEP 6: If the CF ends in a point, fasten off the stitching where it starts to move away from the high hip line, and begin sewing again at an equivalent point on the other side of the CF. Then go back and stitch the CF section, just skimming the top skirt and first few layers of net. If the dancer is partnered, make the stitches small enough to ensure any dance partner cannot trap their fingers in them.

STEP 7: The waist of the basque then needs to be loosely connected to the waist of the bodice on the inside using a chain stitch. Remove the pins from the waist. Use a long cotton four-thread and attach it at the seam allowance closest to the CF.

STEP 8: Take a further small stitch at the waist on top of first stitch – do not pull this stitch tight, but (if you are right-handed) keep the loop it makes in around your right hand and the needle taut in your left.

STEP 9: Now pass your right hand through the loop and grab the taut thread by the needle. Pull this thread through the loop and adjust the tension so that the taut section of thread you have just grabbed becomes the loop, and the previous loop makes a little chain stitch.

STEP 10: Repeat until you have produced a thread chain which is about 2cm long.

STEP 11: Take a small stitch in the basque at the CF waistline underneath the Petersham waistband and pass the needle through the loop to anchor the chain. Pull tight and fasten off using three small stitches. This sounds more complicated than it actually is. The trick is to get the tension correct and your hands working together. Reverse the instructions if you are left-handed. After catching the CF, repeat for the side seams, then the CF/SF seam and the bar side of the SB/CB seam. The chain on the hook side CB/SB seam needs to be a little longer at around 4cm in order to accommodate the bodice extension. Remove the tacking at the waistline.

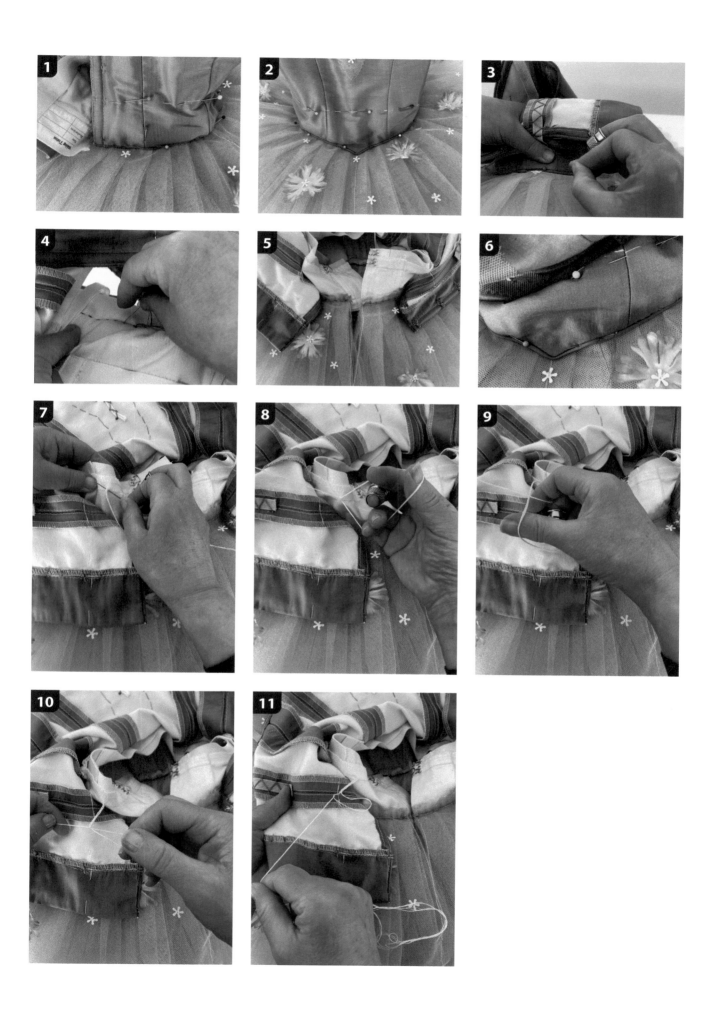

Applying hotfix stones

These are best applied after the costume has been assembled – the finishing touch. The backs of the crystals are covered in glue, which melts at a certain temperature. There is a balance to this: the glue needs to be thoroughly melted, but if it burns it will spoil the adhesive qualities. With this in mind, only warm a few stones at a time. Some people use a wand to apply the crystals. This has a metal 'nib' that collects each crystal individually, melts the glue and the crystal can then be accurately transferred to the costume. I favour a flat-based frying pan on an electric hot plate. While cool, add the crystals to the pan glue-side up, and then place onto the heat source. Do a test on a piece of spare fabric first to check the adhesion: it can be helpful to note the optimum length of time it takes the glue to melt. The crystal gets very hot, so pick it up with the end of a pin and push it into the textile using a thimble or similar protection so the melted glue beds down. If the glue is not hot enough, is burnt or has not been embedded into the cloth, the crystal may drop off.

Think about where you are going to position the stones – do you want to highlight a particular design on a lace fabric? Or do you want a more random effect? It is better to build up the density gradually, working over the whole costume until you achieve the required effect.

Use a pin to transfer the hotfix stones to the garment.

A final check

To finish, remove any tacking and give the costume a final check for any pins that may have been missed.

CHAPTER 8

Extending Your Work and Further Advice

Having established your basic skills, this chapter deals with supplementary processes to expand your practice.

Stretch fabrics

Stretch fabrics are not generally used to make a professional tutu bodice. However, dancers are used to wearing Lycra leotards for class and rehearsal; therefore, it adds comfort if one section like the SB panels are cut in stretch fabric. Nylon Lycra or velvet Lycra work well for bodices on children, as they stretch with them as they grow. To create the pattern, fit a calico toile as before. You will then need to remove what is known as the 'negative ease'. I have found removing an eighth of the circumference at the waist provides a good fit, so if the waist measurement of the toile is 80cm, divide this by eight and subtract. In this case, the finished pattern should measure 70cm at the waist, but the whole panel should also be reduced. You should be aware that if you stretch fabric in one direction, it will contract in the opposite direction, so leave an additional allowance at the top and bottom and check this

at the second fitting. Back the top fabric with ordinary nylon Lycra, and mark this out with dressmaker's carbon paper exactly as with the drill. Then back with the top fabric, but this time there is no need to use the 'push and pin' method.

If using velvet, pay particular attention to the pile – I always cut mine with the pile going up: this way you look into the pile, and the fabric appears dark and rich. Whichever way you choose to have the pile, be accurate with the grain, as any inconsistencies will be especially evident. Make up for the second fitting with the finished tutu, by pinning them together at the waist.

Be careful not to over-fit – if you take too much out of the circumference of the bodice, the textile will take the shortest route, and you can find the fabric will not touch the body at areas like the waist and the curve of the back. Adjust the top and bottom lines as necessary.

Make the bodice up as before, but you may not need to overlock the seam allowances as they will not fray and the stitching is more likely to show from the outside. Use an elastic cord instead of piping cord – a slim hat elastic works well, especially with velvet as the pile will bulk up the result. The piping strip does not need to be cut on the cross as it will stretch anyway. Cut it 3.2mm wide as before, and stitch with a long stitch, folding over a third of the strip and finally overlocking the wider edge.

Dyeing the cotton bobbinet

Dyeing this cotton net is a straightforward process using standard cotton dyes. Begin by washing the bobbinet. Then make up a strong solution of the dye in a glass vessel with a lid (an old jam jar) using hot water, ensuring it is completely dissolved; failure to do this can mean a blotchy final fabric. Add a drop of washing-up liquid to disperse the dye and a tablespoon of salt to fix it. The concentrated dye will keep in the lidded jars if you don't use it all.

To dye the fabric you will need a bowl which is large enough to hold the fabric with room for it to be stirred. Fill it with enough warm water to cover the fabric thoroughly and wet the bobbinet, which will help the dye to disperse evenly. Remove the dampened fabric and set to one side. Add a little of the concentrated dye to the bowl. Test the intensity of the colour with a small scrap of bobbinet. Add the test piece to the bowl, swish it around in the diluted dye, then remove it, rinse it, dry it between kitchen paper and then iron it. Compare the colour of a double layer of the bobbinet to the nylon net you have chosen – if it's too light in tone, add more of the concentrate and test again until you reach the correct intensity. It may be necessary to make concentrates of two different colours if the exact colour is not available to buy. When you are happy with the colour, add the wet fabric. Make sure you keep it moving around the bowl so it gets an even distribution of colour. When the fabric is the right colour, remove it from the bowl and thoroughly rinse it in cold water. Spin dry and while still damp, carefully adjust it back into shape. Iron when dry, making sure the grain is correct.

Machine-stitch the waistline and then pin the high hip line in place.

Covering the basque

You may wish to make a bodice style which finishes on the waist, or only make the tutu plate to use as a rehearsal skirt, for instance, in which case you may decide to cover the basque. If the top fabric is very fine, it may need backing in a fabric like cotton lawn to give it a little more substance.

Make up the basque from drill as described in Chapter 3. Use the same basque pattern and keep it the same at the waist but extend the side seam at the high hip by a total of 12mm. The additional length in the high hip will accommodate the bulk of the tutu and the piping. Add the same seam allowances as before and cut out the top fabric and backing fabric if required. Mark up using dressmaker's carbon paper and if using a backing, machine-tack the two together along the waist, high hip line, CBs and just outside the side seam lines. You will also need to cut enough bias binding to pipe the lower CF and two CB sections. Neaten the side seams at 3cm and the allowance above the waist at 1cm. Pipe the lower edges in three sections, and then the CF and two CBs. The CB on the right-hand-side should finish exactly on the CB and that on the underlap extends 5cm beyond the CB, similar to piping the high hip line on the bodice. Trim back the seam allowances and press into position. To join the side seams, begin by linking the piping on the lower edge with a hand stitch, stabbing through the ditch in the piping as otherwise it has a tendency to slip out of alignment under the machine. Pin the side seams up to the waist and machine-stitch in place with matching thread. Press the seam open with the iron. Next, join this basque at the waist to the waist of the finished tutu. Fold the CB and CB extensions over the finished ends of the basque at the waist only, making sure they sit well. The most important thing is that the CFs match.

Machine-stitch the waists into place, stretching the elastic when stitching across at the side seams. Now bring down the piped edge over the trimmed bobbinet and net edges of the tutu plate; the ditch of the piping should sit exactly on top of this stitched high hip line. Start pinning at the CF and smooth the fabric around the high hip line all the way to the CB. Make any adjustments necessary to make it sit flat but ensure they are symmetrical.

Tack firmly in place ready to check at the second fitting. Add two corset hooks to the waistband and a size 3 hook and bar at the high hip line. At the fitting, ensure the covering sits smoothly over the drill basque; they sometimes bubble slightly and need adjustment.

Tack firmly in place for the second fitting.

Adding a strip of tape to the front of the knicker to shrink its depth and create the effect of a higher leg.

To complete the tutu plate, any decorative top skirt should be added to the high hip line prior to attaching the basque cover, so stitch this on first, before finally hand-stitching the basque into place. Use a double thread and a backstitch which sits discreetly in the ditch of the piping. If desired the waistband can be covered in the conventional way. Replace the hook and bar at the high hip line.

Creating the look of a higher knicker leg

The ballet aesthetic is for long legs and a shorter body, and to exaggerate this, some dancers like a higher leg line on the knicker, if they feel it is more flattering. Another reason this is requested is it happens to be reflected in the fashion of that time. The number of net layers which need to be sewn in the section between the high hip and front of the leg limits how small the knicker depth can be at that point; any closer than 7mm apart and there is the danger that the net layers could end up being stitched on top of one another, creating a stiff and bulky section, and this needs to be taken into account when drafting the knicker pattern.

However, it is possible to cheat the look of a higher leg after the tutu is finished by stitching a short length of tape to the inside of the knicker and slightly gathering the bobbinet between the highest curve on the knicker leg and the high hip.

What to do if the bodice is too low

If the bodice is a little low, either because you have accidently piped it too low, or you have had to fit a longer-bodied dancer into a costume that wasn't made for them, you can either add a frill of net or lace, or add a strip of minx net to the top line to make the dancer feel more secure. Cut it with the stretch going along its length – it is best to put the dancer into the costume and then pin the band into place on the outside. You can then transfer the markings and make several balance marks where it crosses the seam lines. Use this as your pattern to cut out a double layer of fabric, leaving 1cm on the top edge and a 2.5cm allowance on the lower edge. Mark and stitch the top edge with a small zigzag stitch in polyester thread to allow for stretching. Test the stitch first on some scrap fabric. Trim back to 5mm, clip and edge-stitch the turnings to one side of the net – this will become the wrong side and the process will help to stop the turnings from rolling. Now fold back the top line and machine thread-mark the lower edges where they will join to the top piped edge of the bodice. Hand- or machine-stitch this into place – don't worry if it looks a bit tight: since you have fitted it on the dancer under tension, it will look smooth when worn. Attach the lower raw edge to the inside of the bodice using herringbone stitch or catchstitch.

Adding a minx net panel to extend the height of the bodice.

Fabric-covered straps

You can cover the elastic shoulder straps in a tube of matching bodice fabric. Cut the fabric the length of the shoulder strap established at the fitting + 15cm (2.5cm front seam allowance, 7.5cm back seam allowance, 5cm to accommodate the elastic stretching) × 47mm (double the 12mm elastic + 3mm ease + 20mm seam allowance). Cut the fabric on the straight-of-grain. The chart below shows how to calculate the amount of fabric needed for each strap. Remember to cut two pieces.

Fold in half down the length and machine-stitch 10mm from the edge, backstitching at either end for stability. Press the seam allowance back at this stage and then create the tubes by turning through using a safety pin. Insert the elastics and anchor at each end with a straight machine stitch before neatening the remaining raw edges with a zigzag stitch. These straps look best if the stretch is at the back, so before adding them to the bodice, keep around 75 per cent of their length flat, and then stitch across the width allowing the excess fabric to bunch, which will allow the strap to stretch in movement. Pin the flat section with the 2.5cm allowance onto the front, and the longer 7.5cm length to the back. Then stab-stitch the junctions to the bodice through the ditch in the piping with a cotton four-thread in a matching colour. Now stitch down the excess using herringbone stitch. This may be needed if the strap needs altering.

For children

It is important the design is age-appropriate. Simple shapes and embellishments work best.

Every possible allowance should be made for growth. Details of how to make the bodice from stretch fabric are given above.

If you decide to make a woven fabric bodice, the style that finishes on the waist with a CF point extending to the high hip line and separate covered basque works well. These can be joined with buttonhole elastics on the bodice seams and buttons on the inside waistband to allow for some expansion. Follow the instructions above for covering the basque. Copy the bodice pattern, but redraft the lower edge so it finishes on the waist, adding a point at the front, which also allows for growth as this extra section will increase the bodice coverage without impacting the fit. Extra bars can be added to the CBs on both the bodice and the basque for small adjustments, but for any adjustment more than 3cm, the side seams should be let out or the costume will sit asymmetrically on the body. The patterns include large seam

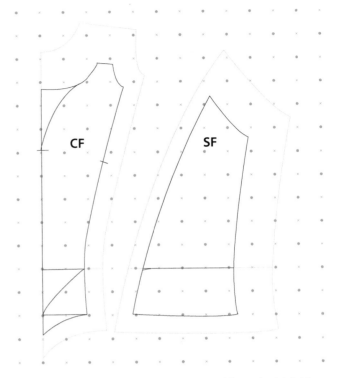

Redrafting the lower edge of the CF panel from the high hip line to the waist.

allowances on the side seams to allow for alteration. The knicker can also be made slightly larger at the high hip line and eased onto the basque; equally, it should stretch a little if the basque needs extending. The excess bobbinet above the high hip line can also be left instead of trimming it back, which will allow it to be dropped on the basque, extending the girth.

Care

Misuse by dancers

When the tutu is complete, and time and effort has been taken to create a specific shape, care of the garment in use is important. Many times, I have witnessed a tutu which has been carefully steamed and ready for the stage being crammed into a tutu bag for transport, or worn backstage and squashed into a lift, or with a heavy bag slung on top of it. Try to discourage this behaviour in young dancers in the hope that, as they get older and their tutus get bigger and less easy to engineer, they will appear on stage as they left the workshop, in as pristine shape as possible.

Cleaning

If you have washed the fabrics (other than the nylon net) before you made the costume, you should not have any problems with shrinkage.

Most professional companies will rinse the knicker section of the tutu base by hand after each performance and give the costume a more thorough clean at the end of a run. A thorough refurbishment should occur every few years to keep the costume in as good condition as possible – the costume will be deconstructed: the bodice and decoration will be removed and washed or professionally dry-cleaned, the boning and stringing stitches will be removed from the base and then the skirt put into a cool washing machine on a gentle cycle. This will then be spun, dried upside down, steamed, re-hooped, reset, restrung, and the costume reassembled. If your costume is to be stored and is not being used for an impending performance, always store it clean and completely dry; sweat and dirt can damage the fibres and make it more liable to rusting and more attractive to infestation!

A less involved way to give your costume a thorough clean is to submerge the whole costume in warm soapy water. You can then gently rub any dirty areas with rubber gloves. Then wrap the rinsed costume in a towel and place flat in a spinner to get rid of most of the excess water. Hang it upside down from the basque hanging loops in a warm place and leave to dry. This inverted hanging guards against the heaviness of the water weighing down the net and should help to revive the shape if it has become a bit droopy.

If you have made a child's costume with a Lycra bodice, you could wash this in a washing machine. First remove any decoration which may get damaged, remove the steel hoop and wash on a gentle setting. Re-hoop the tutu, reset, and restring if necessary.

Storage

A plate tutu is best stored flat. Ensure it is dry and clean, and then wrap the costume in a sheet and place it somewhere it will be undisturbed.

If the costumes are being regularly used, a plate tutu should be hung upside down, using the hanging tapes through the knicker legs; if the tutu is a bell shape, this should be hung the right way up.

If space is an issue, they can be stored in a tutu bag and hung up in a wardrobe. Make sure the loop inside the bag is threaded through the leg hole to provide some support and stop it collapsing within the bag. Under the bed is another effective space-saving storage place.

Tutu bags are an ideal way to transport your tutu. These are readily available, but also easy to make. A duvet cover or sheet also makes a good container in which to transport or store your tutu, but you should avoid folding or crushing your costume. Professional companies will store sets of tutus on a pole – a wide, long wooden pole mounted onto a set of wheels with a flat bed that is the same diameter as a tutu, so when piled with tutus, they can be easily moved around. Special flight cases are used for long-term storage and the tutus are wrapped in muslin.

Conclusion

It takes lots of experience to become a tutu-maker. Maybe not years, but you need to tackle a good quantity of varying sizes and designs before calling yourself a tutu-maker. That said, even the most skilled practitioner will learn and adapt their processes throughout their career. There is no right way to make a tutu, and as with many skills there is flexibility, but there are a few important rules which you need to know before you can break them and develop your own method.

I would suggest anyone contemplating a career in tutu-making should work with at least one established tutu-maker. That way you can see what is involved and if it really is the profession for you. I would also recommend trying to find work experience with a professional ballet company as not only will you get the opportunity to work with dancers, you will also have the chance to have a good look at the costumes that company uses, note their construction and how they differ from others you have seen.

Dance costumes are an engineering feat – they need to be as comfortable as possible, not restrict movement, and look the same when the performance is over as they did when they started. They can be time-consuming to make and the fabrics can be expensive.

But a well-made tutu should be thrilling for a dancer to wear. It should enhance their performance, look light and beautiful, but be comfortable and hard-wearing. Making one and seeing it on stage should give you a real sense of achievement. The first rehearsal of a big new production can be challenging as there is nervous excitement in the air, and as a costume-maker in the theatre on these days you hope no one notices you, praise is not often offered at this point, your services are only needed if there are problems, and on a large set of tutus there are bound to be a few tweaks needed. But do remember the compliments. I once overheard a dancer standing in her brand-new tutu among the flurry of the corps dressing room, looking in the mirror and saying to herself 'I feel incredible', and that I guess is what it's all about.

Amanda Hall, 2024
[Instagram] makingtutusbook

List of Suppliers

Whaleys

Stockist of cotton bobbinet, Amelie (32gsm net), minx net, a good range of cotton calico and drill available in small quantities

Whaleys (Bradford) Ltd
Harris Court
Great Horton
Bradford
West Yorkshire
BD7 4EQ
United Kingdom
Telephone: +44 (0) 1274 576718
Email: info@whaleysltd.co.uk
Website: www.whaleys-bradford.
    ltd.uk

Harrington Fabric and Lace

Stockists of tutu net 4917 with a stiffness rating of 35 and in a good range of colours, 4295 with a stiffness rating of 45, and their stiffest net with a rating of 80 4926, softer nets for the lower layers and leg ruffles, and cotton bobbinet

Online sales or showroom, by appointment
Turret E
Harrington Mills
Leopold Street
Long Eaton
Nottingham
NG10 4QE
United Kingdom
Telephone: +44 (0) 115 946 0766
Email: sales@fablace.co.uk
Website: www.harrington-fabric-
    and-lace.co.uk

Fiorenzatulle S.p.a.

Tutu net – OL40 as stiff net and EVEN for soft net, both in a good range of colours

Via Toscana, 47
59100 Prato (Italia)
P.iva 00398270488
Italy
Website: https://fiorenzatulle.it/en/

Swiss tulle

Bobbinet supplier

Perry Street Works, Factory Lane
South Chard
Chard
Somerset
TA20 2NR
United Kingdom
Telephone: +44 (0) 1460 220312
Email: sales@swisstulle.co.uk
Website: www.swisstulle.co.uk

William Gee

Haberdashery

520–522 Kingsland Road
London
E8 4AH
United Kingdom
Telephone: +44 (0) 207 254 2451
Email: info@williamgee.co.uk
Website: www.williamgee.co.uk

MacCulloch and Wallis

Haberdashery

25–26 Poland Street
London
W1F 8QN
United Kingdom
Telephone: +44 (0) 20 7629 0311
Website: www.macculloch-wallis.
co.uk

Clover

A good range of equipment
including tracing wheels and
marking tools

Available from various suppliers
Website: www.clover-mfg.com

Vena Cava

Suppliers of haberdashery and
costume supplies including a
wide range of boning, both steel
and plastic

Website: www.venacavadesign.co.uk

Richard the Thread

US supplier of haberdashery,
including hooks and bars
Website: www.richardthethread.com

Crystals

Crystal Parade
Online stockists of Preciosa and
Swarovski hotfix crystals
Website: https://crystalparade.co.uk

Burda

Supplier of dressmaker's
carbon paper

Wissner

Suppliers of plastic boning

Website; https://www.wissner.de/en

Mannequins

Suppliers include Kennet & Lindsell
Ltd, Siegal and Stockman, JSF

Morplan

Suppliers of no trace fabric marker
pens and equipment

56 Great Titchfield Street
London
W1W 7DF
Telephone:+44 (0) 20 7636 1887
Website: https://www.morplan.com/
gb_en

Sewing Gem

Online suppliers of sewing
equipment including tutu boning

https://www.sewinggem.co.uk

Fabric Quantities

The following are a guide to the fabric quantities you will need. Check them according to the size and style of tutu you are making. It's most economic if you can work out exactly how much you need, but do be aware that fabric can shrink by up to 10 per cent when washed. You will also need a small amount of spare fabric to test your stitching.

The adult tutu needs very stiff net. Due to the shorter depth of the child's version a net with a tutu rating of 35 will produce a perfectly good tutu.

Quantities for a child's tutu:

For the plate:
0.2m cotton calico or similar for the basque toile
3.5m × 150cm (54in) stiff net
0.5m (approximately) × 150cm (54in) softer net
0.6m × cotton bobbinet 0.5m of 150cm (54in) for the knicker base
0.2m drill or cotton cambric for the basque
2m × 12mm (½in) bias binding for the knicker legs and binding the lower edge of the basque
0.8m × 25mm (1in) wide Petersham for the waistband
20cm (6in) × 25mm (1in) wide elastic for the waistband
1.5m × 7mm wide plastic boning
2 × corset hooks and bars
1 × size 3 dress hook and bar
0.8m × 5mm elastic for the knicker legs
0.4m ribbon for hanging tapes

For the bodice:
0.5m drill for cotton cambric for the bodice backing
1m top fabric for the bodice – allow extra if you want to use the same for the top skirt decoration
Size 3 dress hooks and bars
16cm × 7mm spiral boning for CB
2.5m × size 00 cotton piping cord – shrink before use
0.7m × 12mm elastic for shoulder straps

Quantities for a teen's tutu:

For the plate:
0.2m cotton calico or similar for basque toile
6.5m × 150cm (54in) stiff net
0.5m (approximately) × 150cm (54in) softer net
0.8m × cotton bobbinet 0.5m of 150cm (54in) for the knicker base
0.2m drill for the basque
2.5m × 12mm (½in) bias binding for the knicker legs and binding the lower edge of the basque
1m × 25mm (1in) Petersham for the waistband
20cm (6in) × 25mm (1in) wide elastic for the waistband
2.2m × 7mm fabric-covered steel boning or 7mm wide plastic boning
2 × corset hooks and bars
1 × size 3 dress hook and bar
1m × 5mm elastic for the knicker legs
0.4m ribbon for hanging tapes

For the bodice:
0.7m washed drill for the bodice backing
1.2m top fabric for the bodice – allow extra if you want to use the same for the top skirt decoration
Size 3 dress hooks and bars
17cm × 7mm spiral boning for the CB
3m × size 00 cotton piping cord – shrink before use
1m × 12mm elastic for shoulder straps

Quantities for an adult tutu:

For the plate:
0.2m cotton calico or similar for basque toile
10m × 150cm (54in) stiff net, stiffness rating 40 or more
1m (approximately) × 150cm (54in) softer net
1m × cotton bobbinet 0.5m of 150cm (54in) for the knicker base
0.2m drill for the basque
3m × 12mm (½in) bias binding for the knicker legs and binding the lower edge of the basque
1m × 25mm (1in) wide Petersham for the waistband
20cm (6in) × 25mm (1in) wide elastic for the waistband
2.5m × 7mm wide fabric-covered steel boning
2 × corset hooks and bars
1 × size 3 dress hook and bar
1.2m × 5mm elastic for the knicker legs
0.4m ribbon for hanging tapes

For the bodice:
0.8m washed drill for the bodice backing
1.5m top fabric for the bodice – allow extra if you want to use the same for the top skirt decoration
Size 3 dress hooks and bars
17cm × 7mm spiral boning for CB, add extra for boning the CF or bust seams
3m × size 00 cotton piping cord – shrink before use
1m × 12mm elastic for shoulder straps

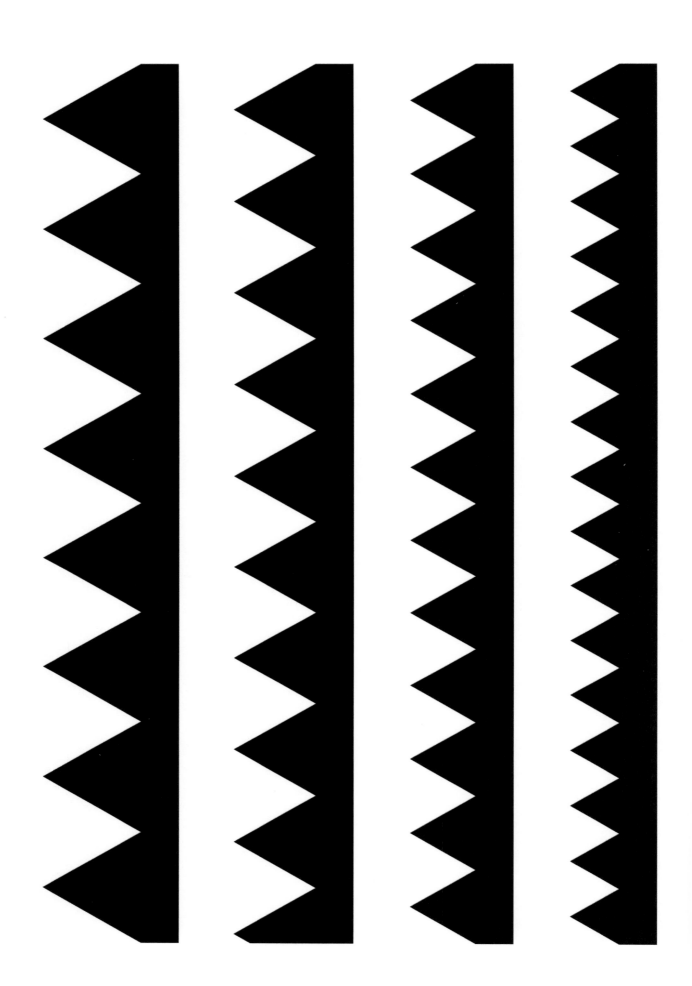

Index

Credits:
Jane Johnson, Phil Reynolds, Eleanor Wilkinson, Melissa
Needham, Fionnuala Quinn, Mal Barton, Fay Fullerton,
Tomoko Honda, and all the enthusiastic tutu-making
students I have taught.
The team who helped put together the RB Swan Lake
corps (2018): Laura, Rosie, Gretchen, Rebekah, Grace,
Sophie, Natasha and the SEC students, and Eleanor,
Hannah, Sophie and Marissa who worked on RB
Cinderella (2023). You all deserve medals.

For Jacqueline, William, Lucy, Susanna and Ali, with
thanks.

First published in 2024 by
The Crowood Press Ltd
Ramsbury, Marlborough
Wiltshire SN8 2HR

enquiries@crowood.com
www.crowood.com

British Library Cataloguing-in-Publication Data
A catalogue record for this book is available from the
British Library.

ISBN 978 0 7198 4314 3

Cover design by Sergey Tsvetkov

Graphic design and typesetting by
Peggy & Co. Design
Printed and bound by CPI Group (UK) Ltd, Croydon, CR0 4YY